Basic Appliqué

1930s Quilt Patterns Created with Traditional and Contemporary Techniques

Cindy Walter & Gail Baker Rowe

Published by

krause publications

700 East State Street • Iola, WI 54990-0001
715/445-2214 • FAX: 715/445-4087   www.krause.com

Please call or write for our free catalog of publications. Our toll-free number, to place an order or obtain a free catalog, is 800-258-0929. Please use our regular business telephone, 715-445-2214, for editorial comment and further information.

Printed in the United States of America.

Library of Congress Catalog Number 2002105752
ISBN 0-87349-347-8

LOST QUILTS:

Gerri Greenblat and Helga Willems each made beautiful quilts for our book. Unfortunately, the quilts were lost in the mail. Gerri's "May Basket" quilt has a strip-pieced background using floral fabrics. Helga made a four-block quilt from the tulip vase pattern. She used a variety of reds for the Tulips. If found, please contact:

Button Box Quilt Shop
Needham, Massachusetts
781-449-9693

Table of Contents

Author's Introduction

From Cindy

Most readers know me best for my popular, contemporary Snippet Sensations technique, but I also love handwork and have taught traditional quilting more than contemporary techniques.

When I first met Gail, she expressed a desire to write a book about 1930 appliqué quilts. I was already planning to write a beginning appliqué book teaching a variety of current techniques, so after talking with Gail I realized that combining our goals into one book would make a perfect and intriguing guide for the beginner.

Cindy Walter

More books from Cindy

From Gail

I've been teaching quiltmaking for many years. I've always had a love for antique quilts, especially the ones from the 1930s with their simplicity and soft colors. And I will admit my heart skips a beat when I see one of these quilts.

When I met Cindy, I was surprised to learn that her background was also in traditional quiltmaking—and that we truly had the same interests in handwork, especially appliqué.

Gail Baker Rowe

From both authors

Even though we live at opposite ends of the United States, we communicate almost daily—mostly by e-mail—and the distance hasn't hindered our desire to bring this book to you.

We both feel the 1930s appliqué blocks are a perfect medium to teach different forms of appliqué techniques; the simple shapes and designs are perfect for the beginner. We know you'll enjoy these historical patterns while, at the same time, learn a variety of appliqué techniques.

We'd like to thank historian Merikay Waldvogel and Mountain Mist for providing us with most of the historical information in this book. And thank you to Maggie Malone for the permission to copy several of the patterns in her book, *Treasury of Applique Patterns*. And a huge thank you to Bettina Havig for the endless inspiration we've acquired from *Carrie Hall Blocks: Over 800 Historical Patterns from the College of the Spencer Museum of Art, University of Kansas*. Also, a special thank you to the talented quilt artists whose quilts are featured in many of the photographs.

*I*ntroduction to *A*ppliqué

Appliqué quilts have always been the epitome of fine quilt making. Pieced quilts are awe inspiring, too, with their bold and graphic designs created by meticulously cutting and seaming the blocks, but appliqué—ah, appliqué—the word itself has a lilting, uplifting quality.

Appliqué is a term used when applying one layer of fabric on top of another. It is one of the oldest techniques, with its roots in quilt making reaching back more than 200 years—and possibly even further, when considering the whole-cloth types of appliqué quilts in India.

You can choose from an endless variety of methods of preparation and ways to stitch appliqué pieces in place. Each method requires different supplies and preparation procedures, which are covered throughout this book.

The patterns we offer are fairly simple, using uncomplicated shapes and layering. They consist of only two or three pieces in some cases. Some appliqué methods are quicker than others; however, there are several variations of these methods. We hope that as you become comfortable with appliqué, you'll explore all of the methods.

*M*ost of the information in this section was provided, or written, by Merikay Waldvogel, a nationally known quilt authority. She is an author, curator, and lecturer focusing on quilts and women's lives. Raised in the Midwest, she first taught English as a Second Language in Chicago and then moved to Knoxville, Tennessee, in 1977, where she co-directed the Quilts of Tennessee project.

Her books include Quilts of Tennessee: Images of Domestic Life Prior to 1930; Soft Covers for Hard Times: Quiltmaking and the Great Depression; Patchwork Souvenirs of the 1933 Chicago World's Fair; *and* Southern Quilts: Surviving Relics of the Civil War.

Merikay is a former board member of the American Quilt Study Group and currently serves on the board of the Alliance for American Quilts.

A Historical Look at the Romance of Applique

"Don't these quilts just seem to open the door to romance? From the fragrant gardens our great-grandmothers grew, it is not much wonder they designed the rare and beautiful old patterns that are real works of art." —Carlie Sexton, Better Homes & Gardens (February 1927)

The album quilts of the mid-1800s not only recorded written sentiments of love and friendship, but they also encapsulated appliqué designs, which had already become somewhat standardized or stylized, based on printed floral motifs on furnishing fabrics.

Red and green, highlighted with pink and yellow, became a favorite color combination for floral appliqué quilts in the 1850s. Pattern names varied from community to community, and even from one decade to another. Many had Biblical or political connotations such as Rose of Sharon and Whig Rose, while others conveyed specific messages of love and affection: Carnation (pure and deep love), Red Rose (I love you), and Violet (faithfulness).

In the South during the Civil War, appliqué quilts were secreted away, often with the family's fine silver inside—a sign of their importance to the woman of the house. After the war, lost or damaged quilts were replicated, producing a revival in the 1870s and '80s of red-and-green floral appliqué quilts.

But pieced-patterned, scrap charm, and crazy patchwork quilts quickly eclipsed the appliqué revival quilts. By the early twentieth century, quilt making was in decline. Crazy quilts and redwork embroidery were wearing on the sensibilities of the "arbiters of good taste."

MARTHA'S VINEYARD – Mountain Mist Pattern #28 ©1931. Martha's Vineyard, 1983, Darlene Scow of Salt Lake City, Utah. The perfectly rounded grapes and beautiful trapunto work make this quilt a favorite of viewers everywhere. Martha's Vineyard is a beautiful quilt design inspired by a half-finished quilt begun in the early 1800s. Mountain Mist Polyester batting. BEST OF SHOW - 1983 MOUNTAIN MIST® QUILT CONTEST. Quilt from the collection of Stearns Technical Textiles, maker of Mountain Mist.

Twentieth Century Appliqué

Enter Marie Webster of Marion, Indiana, whose soft pastel appliqué quilts ushered in a breath of fresh air. The editors of *Ladies Home Journal* called her quilts "The New Patchwork." In its January 1911 issue, the magazine featured four quilts made by Marie Webster, in color no less! The patterns were simple, easily recognizable designs, stripped of any political or Biblical messages: Pink Rose, Snow Flake, Iris, and Wind Blown Tulip.

Later in 1911, the same magazine published nine appliqué designs for cushions by Marie Webster, and in January 1912 Webster's Poppy, Morning Glory, Sunflower, and White Dogwood were published. With a central focus and surrounding borders, Webster's quilts were lovely bedspreads, more decorative than utilitarian. Her floral designs reflected her love of gardening and her artistic training. Her poppy pattern, for example, incorporated the distinct stages in the life of the poppy, from the tightly closed bud to the full-blown bloom, with stems waving in the wind.

Other designers followed Webster's lead, including Anne Orr of Nashville, Tennessee, Mary McElwain of Walworth, Wisconsin, Esther O'Neill of Indianapolis, Indiana, and Mrs. Danner of El Dorado, Kansas. Anne Orr, in particular, showed similar artistic abilities, although Orr was not a quilt maker herself. Like Marie Webster, Anne Orr formed a studio and developed a career based on designing, writing for *Good Housekeeping Magazine*, and selling quilts and pattern booklets through her business in Nashville.

One of our favorite resources for information regarding quilts of this era is the Carrie Hall collection of quilts. This collection of over 800 appliqué and patchwork blocks, made between the period of 1900 and 1935, is in the Spencer Museum of Art at the University of Kansas in Lawrence, Kansas. Carrie Hall was born on December 9, 1866, and in the 1920s, she began collecting quilt blocks. She wanted to find every known pattern, and in 1935 collaborated with Rose Kretsinger to publish *The Romance of the Patchwork Quilt in America*.

None of the quilts from these quilt makers were particularly easy to make. To simplify the process, they offered stamped fabric kits with instruction sheets. The first documented stamped-cloth quilt kit was sold in 1916 (a child's quilt called Kittens). Hundreds of full-size kit quilts were produced, with the most popular flowers being rose, pansy, poppy, and carnation. Smaller-sized appliqué quilts designed for infants and children were also introduced; nursery rhymes were the most popular motifs.

Appliqué Block Patterns

To revive interest in traditional block appliqué designs, Carlie Sexton featured a number of familiar appliqué pattern names in her 1927 article for *Successful Farming*: Rose Sprig, Democratic Rose, and Aunt Dinah's Delight. Two years later, *Farm & Fireside* sponsored a quilt-block contest, which attracted 1,500 blocks as entries. Four of the top winners were red-and-green appliqué designs harkening back to the 1850s. Each printed pattern sheet cost 10 cents to 25 cents each. These printed-paper patterns had very limited instructions, leaving the novice with little chance to succeed without help from an accomplished quilter.

Iris Bed, Mountain Mist pattern #88, 1943, maker unknown. Often the quilters during this period would place colored appliqué pieces on white or solid colored fabrics. Notice the secondary pattern the leaves from the irises create from placing the blocks together without a spacer. Quilt from the collection of Stearns Technical Textiles, maker of Mountain Mist.

Stearns & Foster Co. was somewhat more successful with its line of appliqué Mountain Mist quilt patterns, which mixed old with new. The company's traditional appliqué patterns Rose of Sharon, Princess Feather, and Harrison Rose shared shelf space with the modern, light, and airy Dancing Daffodils, Iris, Martha's Vineyard, Sunflower, and Water Lilies. Today, quilts in these Mountain Mist patterns are often misidentified as kit quilts, when in reality they were made using only a printed pattern sheet.

Besides batting and thread companies and upscale women's magazines, newspapers and farm publications were the main source of quilt patterns for the vast majority of American women in the first half of the twentieth century. In the daily newspapers across the nation, Ruby Short McKim and Florence LaGanke vied for the quilters' attention in the late 1920s and 1930s. McKim had invented the idea of publishing a series of blocks depicting a particular theme (Nursery Rhymes, Circus Animals, etc.), while Florence LaGanke (known to her readers as Nancy Page) wrote and designed similar series blocks for a competing pattern syndicate. *Cappers Weekly, Successful Farming, Farm Journal, Progressive Farmer*, and *Workbasket* also provided syndicated quilt patterns to their subscribers.

This Iris quilt was among the 30 finalists of the Sears Quilt Contest at the 1933 Chicago World's Fair. It was made from an Anne Orr kit, maker unknown. Patchwork Souvenirs (pages 27-28). Photograph courtesy of Merikay Waldvogel.

Some of the popular simple blocks included Sunbonnet Sue, Overall Sam, and Butterflies. Simple appliqué designs arranged in a block grid were easy to make and endearing to hold, but they did not win the prizes at national contests, where judges favored the more stylized appliqué designs. Appliqué kit quilts won top prizes at the 1933 Sears, Roebuck & Company's National Quilt Contest at the Chicago World's Fair. And when Sears offered a bonus prize for a quilt in an original design tied to the theme of the Chicago World's Fair, appliqué was the choice. Just as the gardener who found it surprisingly difficult to render her favorite flower in appliqué, so did the women and men who attempted to depict one hundred years of progress in appliqué for the 1933 Contest.

Appliqué Today

Today's quilt artists still value the traditional patterns and color combinations, but many of the quiltmakers manipulate the colored cloth and thread as an artist mixes her oil paints. The contemporary artist has not only broken away from traditional appliqué colors, layout, and subject matter, they also have freed themselves to express a broader range of emotions.

Our ancestors mostly appliquéd by first thread basting under the raw edges of the pieces, and then blind-stitching the pieces in place. Today, there are many more acceptable methods of appliqué, ranging from heirloom hand stitches to raw edge fusible web. In most quilt shows, appliqué is in a category all by itself, and is either hand- or machine-appliquéd. Extremely detailed appliquéd pictorial scenes are often seen in the innovative categories at these shows.

This book covers the methods of today. We suggest you look at appliqué as two steps—first preparing the piece and then attaching the piece. There are numerous methods of preparing the piece, such as thread basting, freezer paper, drawn lines for needle turn, reversible interfacing, glue stick basting, and applying fusible web. Several of these preparation methods can be interchanged

The Patchwork Quilt

Of all the things a woman's hands have made,
The quilt so lightly thrown across her bed-
The quilt that keeps her loved ones warm-
Is woven of her love and dreams and thread.

When I have spoken to you of its beauty-
"A mere hodge-podge of calico," you said,
"A necessity of homely fashioning,
Just a covering made of cloth and thread."

I knew you'd missed the message hidden there
By hands that fashioned quilts so long ago.
Ambition and assurance are the patches
And the stitches of a quilt are love, I know.

I think a quilt is something very real-
A message of creation wrought in flame;
With grief and laughter sown into its patches
I see beyond the shadows, dream and aim.
Carrie Hall

Page 139 of The Patchwork Quilt, The Romance of the Patchwork Quilt, *Carrie A. Hall and Rose G. Kretsinger, Dover Publications, Inc. New York, Copyright 1935 by the Caxton Printers, LTD. Copyright renewed 1963 by Mrs. L.G. Paxton. Dover Edition, first published in 1988.*

with the three attachment methods of hand stitching, machine stitch, or fusing. In the directional part of this book, we first cover the preparation methods and then tell you which attachment method applies. We then cover the attachment methods.

Today, quiltmakers are not limited by color, design, or availability of fabrics. With the patterns we have presented in this book, the possibilities are endless.

Section 1

Fabric, Tools, and Supplies

The green fabric is from the 1930s. The pink fabric is a reproduction print called Aunt Gracie's from VIP, C Cranston Print Works.

Fabric

Selecting fabric is, without a doubt, one of the most enjoyable aspects of designing a quilt. As you begin to pull fabrics together, the wonderful magic of color begins to emerge. The pastels and soft prints of the 1930s were beautiful, but don't limit yourself to those colors; try bright colors, stripes, or wild theme prints.

To choose your fabrics, audition them by viewing them from a distance or up on a flannel design wall. Be sure to try several combinations; you may be surprised with your final decision.

Not only can you explore the choice of colors used in the appliqué pieces, but you also will begin to realize that background fabric plays an important part in the quilt's overall effect. Don't limit yourself to plain or solid backgrounds. Although a dramatic contrast isn't always needed between the appliqué pieces and the

Old Fashioned Rose, Mountain Mist pattern #22, 1931, maker unknown. These graceful, historical appliqué rose blocks are well proportioned with the narrow, twined stems framing them in the border. When purchasing your fabric, consider buying a little extra in case you want to experiment with designing your own intriguing border treatments. Quilt in the collection of Stearns Technical Textiles, maker of Mountain Mist.

Good contrast

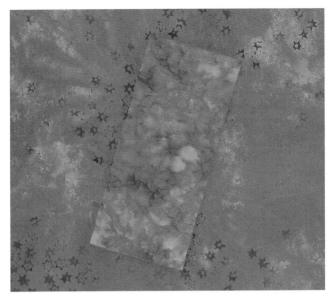

Not good contrast

background, fabric contrast is needed to keep the appliqué pieces from becoming lost. As you choose fabrics, remember that contrast can be achieved not only with color, but also with the fabric's print scale.

Any kind of fabric can be used for appliqué, except when using the fusible web method, as described on page 15. When using fusible web, the fabric needs to be able to be ironed to set the web (different brands require different ironing times), so test the fabric first if you have any doubts.

When hand stitching appliqué pieces, we prefer cotton and silk fabrics, because they have a light hand, making it easier to "sink," or hide, the appliqué stitch. Heavy fabric, such as denim, is harder to hand appliqué, but will work fine if you are machine appliquéing.

Regardless of which type of fabric you use, be sure to pre-wash it to remove any chemicals used in the milling process, to remove excess dyes, and to give the fabric a softer feeling. When pre-washing the fabrics, do not add more chemicals—use special fabric soaps available at quilt or fabric shops, or a commercial phosphate-free soap.

Tools and Supplies

Here, we summarize all of the supplies used in this book; note that each appliqué method uses slightly different supplies. The appliqué method you choose may not use all of the supplies referred to in this section. Please carefully read through the supply lists in each of the method sections before beginning any project.

The tools and supplies are listed alphabetically. Remember, not all supplies are used for all methods.

Appliqué Pins

We suggest using small appliqué pins, 1/2" or 3/4" long, when hand appliquéing. The thread will not catch as easily on shorter pins. For machine appliqué, you can also use appliqué pins, or use regular sewing pins. The brands we like include Bohin, Clover, Foxglove Cottage, and John James, because they are sharp and sturdy. Pins are useful in all methods of appliqué.

Bias Bars

Bias bars are handy for turning under the edges on long, thin stems. They come in all sizes and are made from several materials. We prefer metal bars from the Celtic Design Company, because you can achieve a sharper fold when pressing against their metal edges. Be sure to follow the package directions. Bias bars are useful in all methods of appliqué when the pattern has a long stem—except for the fusible web method; in that case, you are not turning under the edges.

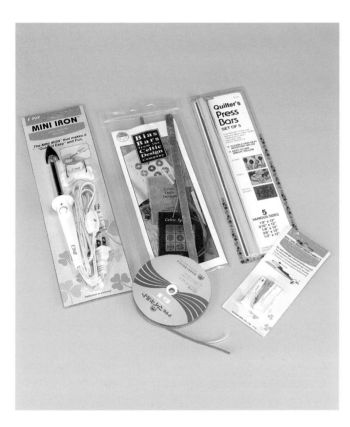

Freezer Paper

Freezer paper is used for two methods in this book. It acts as a template to show you the seam allowance lines. To create the freezer paper template, you simply trace the pattern on the paper side with a pencil, cut it out, and then temporarily iron the shiny side to the fabric.

Fusible Interfacing and Wash Away Stabilizer

Fusible interfacing is only used in one method in this book. Wash-away stabilizer can be used in place of the interfacing. This method is a fast way to turn under the seam allowance, but only works well on larger pieces with smooth edges. Interfacing that isn't fusible also works, but we prefer the fusible feature to temporarily hold the appliqué piece to the block while hand or machine stitching. The brands we prefer include, HTC Inc. FUSIBLE Non-Woven Interfacing and Pellon FUSIBLE® NONWOVEN INTERFACING. For stabilizer, we prefer Pellon's Sol-U-Web™ and HTC Inc. RinsAway™.

Fusible Web

Fusible web is only used for one method in this book. You do not turn under the edges when using fusible wed; the appliqué piece is simply cut to size after the web has been attached and then ironed into place.

Many fusible webs are currently available. Read the different webs' package directions carefully, because they vary greatly. We prefer Steam-A-Seam2, because it is so easy to use. Its pressure-sensitive feature temporarily adheres to the appliqué piece and, in turn, also temporarily adheres to the background fabric. Once the block is finished, you simply iron the web for 15 seconds in each area to make the temporary bond permanent. We also recommend a new web called Lite Steam-A-Seam2 for its soft hand. Note that templates are not used for the fusible web method, because web is transparent, and the pattern pieces can be traced directly onto it.

Untitled

My neighbor is washing her windows,
And scrubbing and mopping her floors,
But my house is all topsy and turvey,
And the dust is behind all the doors.

My neighbor, she keeps her house spotless,
And she goes all day at a trot;
But no one would know in a fortnight
If she swept today or not.

The task I am at is enticing–
My neighbor is worn to a rag–
I am making a quilt out of pieces
I saved in a pretty chintz bag.

And the quilt, I know my descendants
Will exhibit with credit to me –
"So lovely – my grandmother made it
Long ago in 1933."

But will her grandmother remember
Her struggles with dirt and decay?
They will not – they will wish she had made them
The quilt I am making today.
Cynicky Phin

Clipping from newspaper found on p. 99, column 3 "Patchwork Quilts" (Scrapbook #1) Carrie Hall Collection, Spencer Museum, Lawrence, Kansas, page 10, *Carrie Hall Blocks*, Bettina Havig, Copyright 1999, AQS, Paducah, Kentucky.

Glue

Glue is only used in one method of appliqué where the glue is used to hold under the seam allowance. There are several types on the market, but we prefer Roxanne's appliqué glue or a regular glue stick.

Marking Pens and Pencils

For all appliqué methods you will need a quilter's pencil, or regular lead pencil, to mark on template plastic, cardboard, fusible web, or freezer paper, as well as fabric. If you can't see the pencil lines on your fabric, try a quilter's white lead or chalk pencil.

When marking on a vinyl placement guide, however, be sure to use a permanent pen, such as a Sharpie.

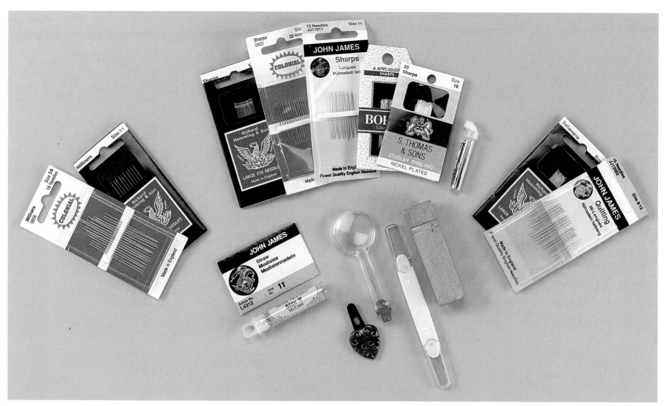

A variety of needles and needle threaders.

Needles

The most common needle used for hand appliquéing is called a Sharp; we recommend a size 10 or 11. This needle has a very thin shaft and a sharp point, making it ideal for appliqué work. Milliner, Straw, and Betweens are also used in size 10 or 11. All of these needles have sharp points and thin shafts, but they vary in length. You might try several sizes before finding a needle size that you prefer.

These needles are only used for hand attaching the appliqué pieces to the base, not in machine appliqué or fusible web methods.

*G*ail finds the longer needles, called Milliners or Straws, more comfortable to handle. She also prefers these longer needles when teaching beginners the needleturn method.

*C*indy is more comfortable using a shorter needle, either a Sharp or a Between.

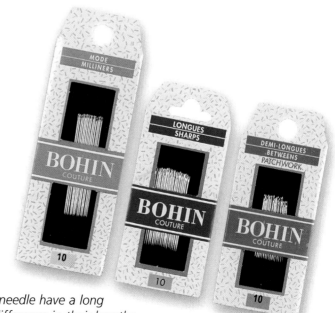

All three of these basic types of needle have a long shaft and sharp tip. Notice the difference in their lengths.

Placement Guide Material and Permanent Pen

For all of the appliqué methods, you will find that a piece of clear vinyl, or other semi-transparent guide including tracing paper, is a great help to you when placing appliqué pieces on a background. This will be especially helpful if you are making more than one block; all of the blocks will be identical. Clear vinyl can be obtained from any large fabric shop.

Template Material and Pencil

You can find sheets of plastic template material, also known as Mylar, at most quilt and fabric shops. While cardboard, or other hard surfaces you can cut out, can also serve for templates, we recommend that you use plastic template sheets because they are transparent, easy to work with, and inexpensive. Note that you do not need to make templates for the fusible web method.

Scissors

You should always keep a variety of scissors handy. We use three different pairs: old scissors to cut out vinyl, cardboard, or plastic template material; sharp fabric scissors for cutting fabrics; and small scissors to clip threads and curves while appliquéing. Also, rotary cutting equipment is handy when cutting out large squares of vinyl and background fabrics.

Sewing Machine and Basic Sewing Supplies

It is completely possible to create a quilt without a sewing machine by hand appliquéing, hand piecing, and hand quilting. But, most people will choose to use a machine for at least one of the steps.

The type of machine you need varies on your goals. If you plan to appliqué by hand and then piece the blocks together by machine, you will only need a basic machine with straight stitching. But, if you plan to create decorative machine appliqué stitches, you will need a higher-end machine. Make sure your machine is in good working order.

Thimble

A thimble of some type is needed to protect the finger that helps to push the needle while thread basting or hand appliquéing. We suggest that you wear a thimble on the middle finger of your sewing hand. Metal sewing or quilting thimbles are wonderful, but you can also use those made of leather, some of which are designed for long fingernails. Cindy wears a metal concave quilting thimble, while Gail wears an antique silver sewing thimble.

The machine appliqué stitch, on the other hand, is usually meant to show; such a stitch gives you more options for the types of threads you can use. We prefer using 40 wt. cotton thread and avoid "temperamental" ones, such as metallic. Clear monofilament nylon thread can also be used, although it might lend a stiff feeling to the quilt. We explore a variety of stitches in the machine appliqué section. Try using a contrasting color of thread and allowing the stitch to become a major part of the overall appliqué design.

Threads

Different types of threads are used, depending on whether you appliqué by hand or by machine.

One goal of hand appliqué is to render the stitch almost invisible. Invisible stitches can be achieved by matching the thread color to the appliqué piece (not the background fabric), taking tiny "bites" out of the appliqué piece, and by using a thin thread that will "sink" into the fabric. Lightweight (60 wt.) cotton is the preferred thread for the hand appliqué stitch. Avoid thicker cotton threads, such as those designed for hand quilting or machine piecing, because their thicker nature renders them difficult to hide in the appliqué stitch. Silk (100 wt.) is also suitable because the thread is easy to hide.

Section
2

Getting
Started

There are several methods to prepare an appliqué piece before attaching it to your background. The preparation methods covered in this book are hand basting, needleturn, freezer paper on top, freezer paper on bottom, fusible web, reverse interfacing, and appliqué glue. We encourage you to try all of the methods to determine which one you like the most.

We introduce the preparation methods in the order of the most traditional to the most contemporary. Thread basting is the most traditional method of preparation. Cindy teaches this method in her classroom; however, she varies the method she personally uses, depending on the type of project she is making. The next most traditional method is needleturn. This is Gail's favorite method because she can work fast and accurately. It is also the method of appliqué made famous by the Hawaiians. An old standard method uses freezer paper. Gail teaches the freezer paper on the topside of the fabric with the needleturn method in her classroom because the paper edge makes a good guide for the beginner.

There is also a method using the freezer paper on the wrong side of the fabric. The newest methods are glue stick, reversible interfacing, and fusible web. Some of these preparation methods can only be attached in a specific way, which we explain thoroughly in each section. We cover all of the preparation methods before teaching you the attachment methods.

Once the appliqué piece is prepared, there are three primary ways to attach it to the background fabric: Hand stitching, machine stitching, and adhering with fusible web. Remember certain preparation methods match certain attachment methods, and we clearly outline them in each section.

There is basic information that applies to all forms of appliqué. Regardless of the method of you choose, you will need to know the following information about patterns, placement guides, templates, preparing the background block, and working order. So, let's explore the basic information you will need to know before talking about the different appliqué and attachment methods.

Patterns

The appliqué patterns in this book are printed in the finished size, without seam allowances. Most of the preparation methods turn under the edges of the pieces; in this case you will need to add the seam allowance to the pattern measurements.

❖ Add 1/4" seam allowance for the thread basting and reversible interfacing methods.

❖ Add a generous 1/8" inch seam allowance for needleturn, freezer paper, and the glue stick method.

❖ Do not add seam allowances for the fusible web method.

The pattern pieces are numbered so you will know how many of each piece you will need to cut from the fabric for each block

The numbers on the small diagrams on the project pages indicate the placement order.

Notice that several of the patterns are split in half, or are quartered, to fit on the pages. Be sure to trace and rotate them to create a complete pattern and pattern elements.

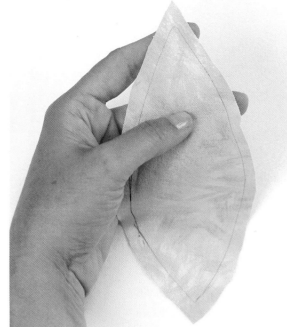

In preparation for thread basting, we added a 1/4" seam allowance to the piece. Do this by cutting the template to the finished size and add the seam allowance when cutting the fabric.

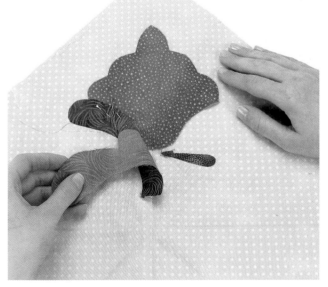

When pieces overlap, do not turn under the seam allowance on the hidden area of the piece on the bottom; doing so will help prevent excess bulk.

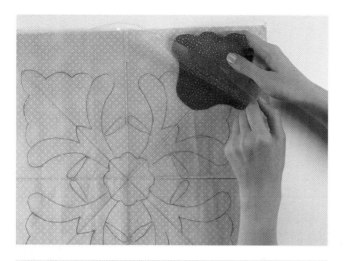

Placement Guide

A placement guide will assist you in putting appliqué pieces in the correct spots on the background fabric. For all of the appliqué methods described in this book, we encourage you to make a placement guide, especially if you are making more than one block of the same pattern; the blocks then will be identical. To the left, we are sliding the appliqué piece under the guide to the correct position.

For the placement guide, you can use vinyl, tissue paper, tracing paper, or a light box. We prefer lightweight vinyl (available at most fabric and craft shops), because it is transparent and does not tear. It is very important to use a permanent ink pen when drawing on vinyl. A regular pen will bleed when damp and ruin the fabric. Save the vinyl's original packaging tissue to store the placement guide to prevent permanent ink from rubbing off.

To make your placement guide, cut the vinyl the same size as the unfinished block. Using a ruler and the permanent pen, draw vertical, horizontal and two diagonal lines through the center of the vinyl placement guide. Mark "TOP" in a corner, so you won't reverse the vinyl.

Place the vinyl, using the drawn lines to guide you, over the pattern you have chosen. In most cases, one fourth of the pattern is given. Repeat tracing the pattern until you have a complete pattern on the vinyl.

Templates

We suggest that you make re-use-able templates to prepare appliqué pieces for all the methods in this book, except for the fusible web method. The templates can be made from any firm object—such as cardboard or Mylar plastic template sheets—so you can trace around their perimeter to mark the appliqué motifs on top of the fabric, or on the freezer paper. We use the Mylar plastic template sheets because they have a firm edge. The templates are the finished size of the appliqué patterns, and the seam allowance is added to the fabric when cutting it out. Write the pattern name on the top of the template pieces with a permanent ink pen.

To make a template out of plastic, set the plastic on top of the appliqué pattern and trace one of each of the pattern's design shapes. Cut out on the line with old scissors.

To make a template out of cardboard, photocopy the appliqué pattern, cut out one of each of the pattern's motifs, and trace or glue it on top of the cardboard. Then cut out the cardboard template on the traced lines of the pattern with old scissors. For a large quilt, you may have to make several templates of the same pattern piece because the edges of the cardboard will become worn, and the template will no longer be accurate.

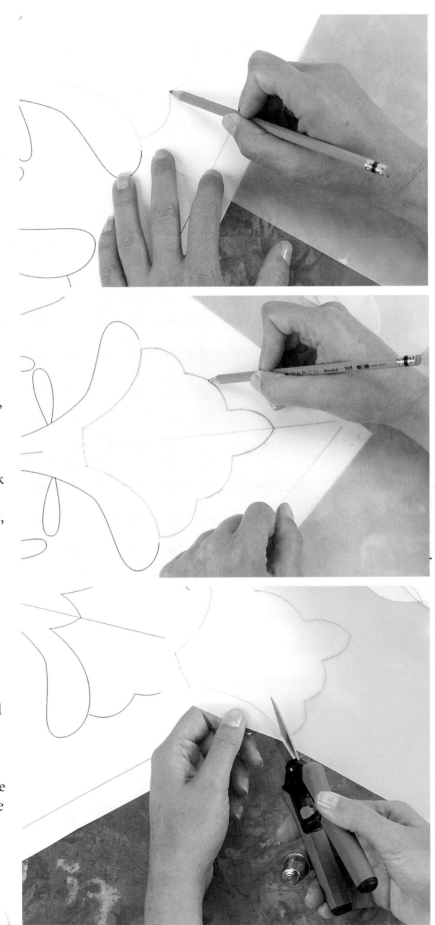

Background Fabric Blocks

The appliqué patterns in this book are applied on top of squares of background fabric. This block method of constructing a quilt was very popular in the early part of the nineteenth century. The patterns do not have to go on individual blocks; you could also appliqué them on anything such as a whole cloth, garment, or even placemats.

To assist with the placement of the appliqué pieces, press each square in half vertically, open it up, and then press horizontally; open and press diagonally, and then open and press diagonally in the final direction. You will now have four pressed lines on the background block that match the drawn lines on the placement guide.

Working Order

Many appliqué patterns are built with layers, creating a three-dimensional effect. To achieve the proper layering in the appliqué blocks, our line diagrams have been numbered with the working order sequence. Begin with the pattern pieces labeled #1; attach all #1 pieces in place before continuing with the pieces labeled #2, and so on.

Stems and Bias Bars

Several of the blocks have stems. You do not need a special tool to make these thin strips although it makes the process easier. There are several tools available. We prefer the Celtic Bars; we show you how to use these in the photograph. The width of the strips of fabric cut on the bias for these stems varies. Follow the guidelines given for cutting, sewing, and ironing the fabric on the bias strip's packaging.

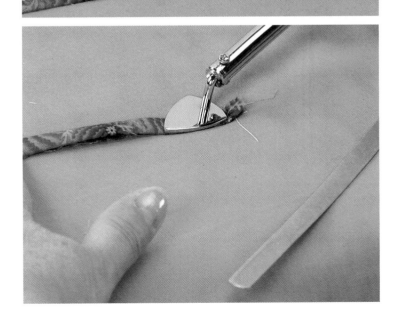

Section 3

Appliqué

Preparation Methods

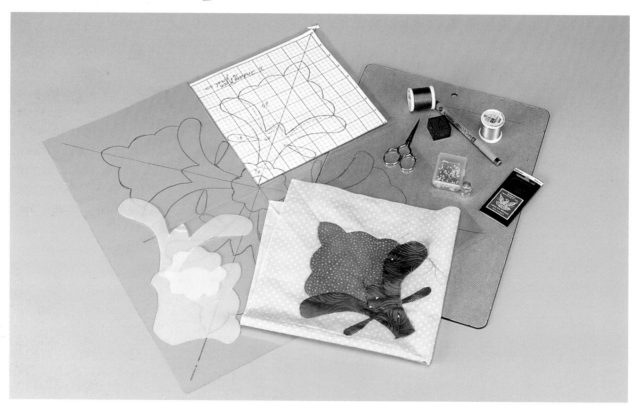

You are now ready to get started. Read the following appliqué preparation methods to understand the different styles. Then, choose the style you'd like to try. Notice each style has its own unique set of supplies. Some styles must be hand stitched, while others can be hand stitched, machine stitched, or fused.

Thread Basting

Thread basting is one of our historical, tried-and-true methods of turning under the edges of the appliqué pieces before attaching them to the block. The edges are turned under by hand, and temporarily held in place with a running basting stitch of thread. After the piece is attached to the background block, the basting thread is removed. This method can be attached to the background fabric either by hand or machine appliquéing.

You Will Need
❖ Placement guide
❖ Template plastic
❖ Scissors, old and good
❖ Pencil
❖ Thimble
❖ Needle
❖ Regular cotton thread
❖ Applique pins

1 Make a placement guide, following the instructions on page 22.

2 Make a template for each of the numbered pattern pieces, following the instructions on page 23.

3 Set the templates on the right side of the corresponding fabrics. Leaving at least 1/2" between each piece, trace with a pencil or wash-away fabric pen. Trace the number of pieces needed for the entire project.

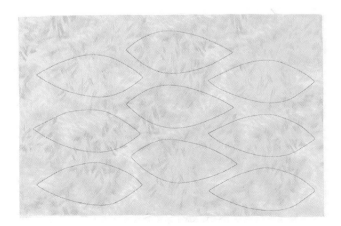

4 Using sharp scissors cut out each piece, adding a 1/4" seam allowance around the outside of the traced line.

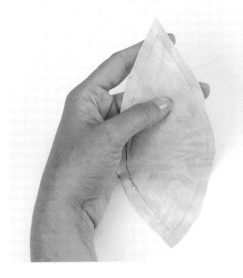

5 Clip any inside curves up to, but not across, the stitching line.

6 Make a double knot in the basting thread. Working from the top of the fabric, turn under the seam allowance of a small portion of the appliqué piece, and hold it under with your fingers. Stick the needle in through the top of the piece, about 1/8" from the folded edge, catching the turned-under seam allowance, while leaving the knot sitting on top of the fabric. Make a running stitch with the basting thread through the turned-under seam allowance.

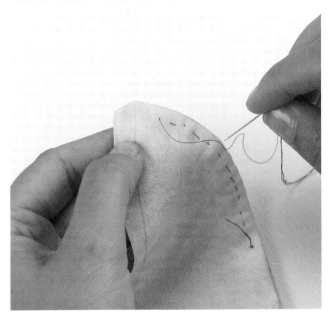

Continue turning under small amounts of the seam allowance and basting the edges under as you turn them.

End the basting stitch on the top by clipping the thread about 1" long. Do not knot. Remember to not turn under the seam allowance on areas that will be layered under other appliqué pieces.

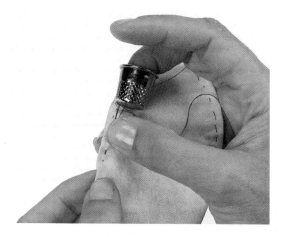

You can load the needle with quite a few stitches.

7 Following the sequence working order, pin the pieces marked #1. Hand or machine appliqué the pieces to the background.

8 Once the piece is stitched in place to the background, simply remove the basting thread by grabbing and pulling on the knot.

Always leave the basting thread knot on the top of the piece so you can easily pull it from the piece. To make it easier to see the basting stitches, use a thread that contrasts against the color of the fabric.

Needleturn Preparation

The needleturn method is another traditional and efficient way to appliqué. Here, you are actually preparing the piece and then hand appliquéing it to the background as you turn under the seam allowance;, in the thread basting method you are just holding it in place. After drawing the seam allowance on the top of the appliqué pieces, you will pin the pieces to the background, and then turn under the seam allowance with the tip of the needle before making a blind appliqué stitch.

This method is attached to the background by hand appliqué only.

Chrysanthemum by Elizabeth Root
The makers of world-renowned Hawaiian quilts use the needleturn method of appliqué. You can find the pattern for this beautiful quilt in Pillows to Patch Quilt Collection...the Hawaiian Way, *by Elizabeth Root.*

You Will Need

❖ Placement guide
❖ Template plastic
❖ Scissors, old and good
❖ Pencil (or brown Pigma or fine point-
  ed permanent marker)
❖ Appliqué pins

Step 5

1 Make a placement guide, following the instructions on page 22.

2 Make a template for each of the numbered pattern pieces, following the instructions on page 23.

3 Place the templates on the right side of the corresponding fabric. Try to place the edges of the templates on the bias of the fabric (a bias edge turns under easier than a straight of grain edge). Leaving at least 1/2" between each piece, trace with a fine-point pencil or permanent pen. Trace the number needed for your pattern.

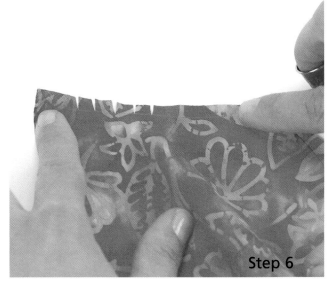

Step 6

4 Cut out the pieces, adding a generous 1/8" seam allowance all around.

5 Clip any inside curves up to, but not across, the stitching line. Finger press the seam allowance under.

6 Using the placement guide, place the first pattern pieces marked #1 on the background block. (By following the working order you will work in stages, securing one layer at a time.)

7 Using several pins, secure the center of each piece without letting the pins overlap the stitching line.

8 You are now ready to hand appliqué. You will now need to turn to page 43 and follow the directions for the needleturn version of hand appliqué stitch.

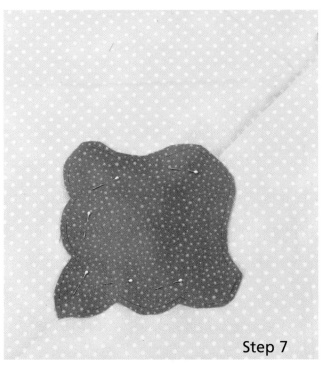

Step 7

Freezer Paper on Top

Gail prefers the freezer paper on top method of appliqué when teaching, because the freezer paper serves as a good guide for the beginner. It is also a favorite of master appliquér Ellie Sienkiewicz; we highly recommend Ellie's books because of their wonderful patterns—we've listed them in the Recommended Reading section.

This method is a rendition of the needleturn method, except that a freezer paper template is used instead of a drawn line. So, just like needle-turn, this is a method that requires you to prepare the piece and then hand appliqué it to the background as you turn under the seam allowance.

This method is attached to the background by hand appliqué only.

You Will Need

❖ Placement guide
❖ Template plastic
❖ Freezer paper
❖ Ironing equipment
❖ Scissors, old and good
❖ Pencil
❖ Pins

1 Make a placement guide, following the instructions on page 22.

2 Make a template for each of the numbered pattern pieces, following the instructions on page 23.

3 Set the templates on the paper side of the freezer paper. With a pencil, trace the number needed for your pattern; you will need a freezer paper pattern for each applique piece of the quilt. Cut out the pieces on the traced line.

4 Working on a hard ironing surface, place the shiny side of the freezer paper pieces on the right side of the corresponding fabric. Make sure they are at least 1/2" apart in every direction. Press each freezer paper piece with a hot, dry iron until it is well adhered to the fabric; you may have to press several times to ensure the paper is completely adhered to the fabric.

Gail wraps a piece of cotton batting around an empty cardboard fabric bolt and uses it for her ironing board when adhering freezer paper templates. This hard surface works better than an ironing board.

5 Cut out the pieces, adding a generous 1/8" seam allowance all around.

6 Clip any inside curves up to, but not across, the stitching line. Finger-press the excess seam allowance to the wrong side of the piece.

7 Using the placement guide, place the first pattern pieces marked #1 on the background block. (By following the working order, you will work in stages, securing one layer at a time.)

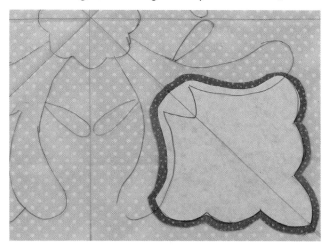

8 Securely pin the center of each piece, without letting the pins overlap the stitching line.

9 You are now ready to hand appliqué. You will now need to turn to page 43 and follow the directions for the needleturn version of the hand appliqué stitch. If you have a problem removing the freezer paper after appliquéing, warm the surface of the paper with an iron; you will then be able to remove it easily. Here, we have started to needleturn.

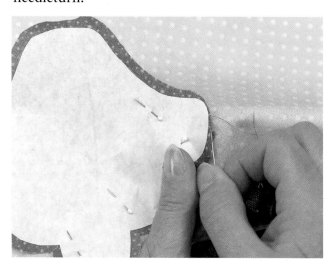

Freezer Paper Inside

The freezer paper inside method is another popular way to use freezer paper. Here, the paper is pressed to the wrong side of the fabric, and then the seam allowance is either pressed or thread basted over the freezer paper.

For this method, attach pieces to the background by hand or machine appliqué.

You Will Need

❖ Placement guide
❖ Template plastic
❖ Freezer paper
❖ Ironing equipment
❖ Scissors, old and good
❖ Pencil
❖ Pins

1 Make a placement guide, following the instructions on page 22.

2 Make a template for each of the numbered pattern pieces, following the instructions on page 23.

3 Set the templates on the paper side of the freezer paper. With a pencil, trace the number needed for your pattern. You will need a freezer paper pattern piece for each applique piece of the quilt. Cut out the pieces on the traced line.

4 Working on a hard ironing surface, place the shiny side of the freezer paper pieces on the wrong side of the corresponding fabric. Make sure they are at least 1/2" apart in every direction. Press each freezer paper piece with a hot iron until it is well adhered to the fabric; you may have to press several times to ensure the freezer paper is completely attached to the fabric.

5 Cut out the pieces, adding a scant 1/4" seam allowance all around.

6 Clip any inside curves up to, but not across, the stitching line. Fold under the seam allowances toward the freezer paper and secure by finger pressing and ironing.

7 Using the placement guide, place the first pattern pieces marked #1 on the background block. (By following the working order, you will work in stages, securing one layer at a time.)

8 Securely pin the center of each piece without letting the pins overlap the stitching line.

9 You are now ready to hand or machine appliqué the piece to the background, following the directions on pages 43-46.

10 When you reach about 1" from the end of securing each piece to the background, pull out the freezer paper, and finish stitching. You can also complete the appliqué and then make a small slit behind it. Pull out the freezer paper from the back using tweezers. This slit needs to be closed with a few stitches.

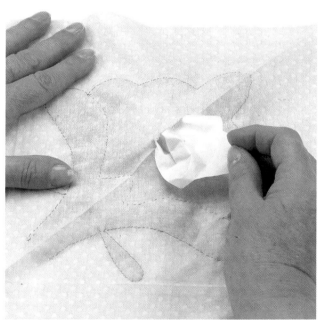

Interfaced Lined Appliqué

In the interfaced lined appliqué method, a fusible liner of interfacing or stabilizer is used to flip the appliqué piece right side out, leaving the raw edges turned to the inside. Once attached to the background base, depending on whether you use interfacing or stabilizer, it will either remain in place or wash away.

This method is best used for larger pieces, not smaller ones with intricate shapes.

Once fused in place, this method is attached to the background by hand or machine appliqué.

You Will Need

❖ Placement guide
❖ Template plastic
❖ Fusible interfacing or stabilizer
❖ Ironing equipment
❖ Scissors, old and good
❖ Pen or permanent marker
❖ Pins
❖ Knitting needle or pointed tool
❖ Sewing machine

1 Make a placement guide, following the instructions on page 22.

2 Make a template for each of the numbered pattern pieces, following the instructions on page 23.

3 Set the templates on the wrong side of the corresponding fabric. With a pencil or permanent ink pen, trace the number needed for your pattern. Make sure they are at least 1/2" apart in every direction.

4 Set the whole piece of fabric on the fusible interfacing, placing the web side of the interfacing to the right side of the fabric. You will have the wrong side of the fabric on the top, and the non-web side of the interfacing on the bottom. Place a pin in the center of each appliqué piece.

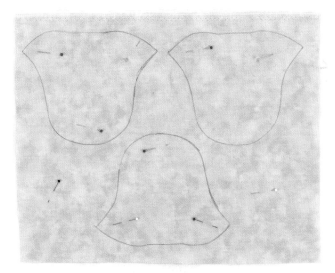

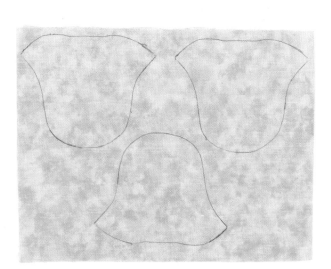

5 Sew on the traced line around each appliqué piece, sewing the fusible interfacing to the fabric.

6 Once sewn, cut out the pieces, adding a scant 1/4" seam allowance all around.

Turn the piece inside out. Use a dull point, such as a knitting needle, to coax out the edges. Now you have perfectly basted under seams.

7 Clip any inside curves up to, but not across, the stitching line.

8 Pull the interfacing away from the fabric and make a tiny slit in the center of the interfacing.

9 Using the placement guide, place the first pattern pieces marked #1 on the background block. (By following the working order, you will work in stages, securing one layer at a time.)

10 If you are using a fusible interfacing, fuse the pieces in place by pressing them with a hot iron, following the interfacing package directions. If you are using stabilizer, secure the pieces to the background with appliqué pins.

11 You are now ready to hand or machine appliqué the piece to the background, following the directions on pages 43-46.

This is Cindy's favorite method for large appliqué pieces like the petals on the White Lily quilt she made for her book, **The Basic Guide to Dyeing & Painting Fabric.**

Fusible Web, Raw Edge

The fusible web method with raw, unturned edges is a favorite appliqué method for the contemporary quilter because it is so fast.

Although there are many webs on the market, we strongly recommend Steam-A-Seam2, because it is easy to use and creates a permanent bond. For bed quilts, we recommend the new Lite Steam-A-Seam2; in addition to having all of the attributes of regular Steam-A-Seam2, it has a very soft hand and washes beautifully.

This preparation method is secured to the background fabric by ironing—but it can be embellished by machine appliquéing.

You Will Need

❖ Placement guide
❖ Fusible web
❖ Ironing equipment
❖ Scissors, old and good
❖ Pencil

Steam-A-Seam2 has release paper on each side of the web. During manufacturing, the web is applied to one of these papers so it is more securely attached to that piece. Check which paper is the one more firmly attached and trace on that piece of paper.

1 Make a placement guide, following the instructions on page 22.

2 Set the web on top of the pattern; trace the number needed for each pattern piece with the pencil. Group the numbered pieces together on the web, so they can be applied to the corresponding fabric in a whole sheet.

3 Pull off the side of the paper on which you have not traced, exposing the web.

4 Set the web on the wrong side of the corresponding fabric. Firmly press it on to the fabric with your hand; the web is pressure-sensitive and will temporarily adhere to the fabric.

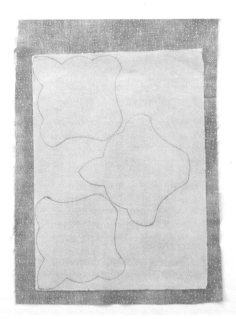

5 Cut out each piece, following the traced seam lines on the fusible web's paper.

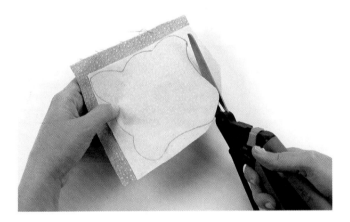

6 Using the placement guide, set the first pattern pieces marked #1 on the background block. (By following the working order, you will work in stages, securing one layer at a time.) Be careful to not touch the vinyl placement guide with your hot iron because it will melt.

7 Once the pieces for an entire block are in place (or you have an amount that easily fits on your ironing surface), press with a hot steam iron for 15 seconds in each area. If you are using a web other than Steam-A-Seam2, be sure to carefully follow the package instructions.

8 Once the pieces have been fused, you can embellish with a machine appliqué stitch.

Fusible webs do not adhere well to some chemicals used in the milling process. It is advisable to pre-wash your fabric and not use fabric softeners in the washing machine or dryer. If you are using Steam-A-Seam2 and your fabric does not stick to the pressure-sensitive web, slightly warm the fabric with an iron to keep it in place.

The Bouquet, 9-3/4" x 11-1/4", 2000, Jessie Harrison. Jessie said, "This bouquet was designed so I could do several of my favorite things: miniature appliqué, 3-D flowers, trapunto, and hand quilting." This award-winning quilter used a variation of the glue stick method when working with miniature pieces. She cleverly designed the patterns on a computer, and then printed them on label paper (instead of freezer paper). The world lost this extremely talented quilter at the end of 2001. The quilt is in the private collection of the Harrison Family Trust.

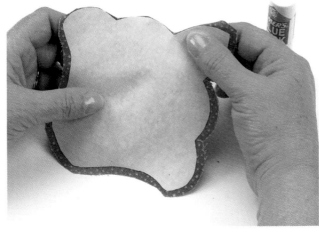

Glue Stick

Contemporary quilters use two new methods of preparing an appliqué piece with a glue stick. These glue stick preparation methods allow the pieces to be secured to the background fabric either by hand or machine appliquéing. Once the appliqué piece is secured to the base fabric, wash the project to remove the glue.

For the first glue stick method, follow the supplies and directions for the Freezer Paper on Top method, as explained on page 31. Instead of needleturning the edges under while appliquéing it to the base fabric, however, first hold the raw edges under with the glue stick. Appliqué the piece to the background block, either by hand or machine stitching.

For the second glue stick method, follow the supplies and directions for the Freezer Paper on the Inside method (page 33). You will be using a stabilizer, such as HTC's RinsAway™ stabilizer, instead of freezer paper.

To use RinsAway, bond two pieces by misting with water and pressing them together for a double thickness. Trace the appliqué pattern on the stabilizer, and cut out the finished size of the appliqué piece. Place it on the wrong side of the fabric and cut out the fabric, leaving a 1/4" seam allowance. Fold the seam allowance over the edges of the piece, and use the glue stick to secure it.

You are now ready to appliqué the pieces in place, either by hand or machine appliqué. Although the RinsAway has the stiffness of a manila folder, you do not have to remove it before attaching an appliqué piece to the base, because it will disappear once you wash the quilt. Deb Wagner is a fan of this technique. For additional appliqué ideas we recommend Deb's book *Traditional Quilts Today's Techniques*.

Either method is attached to the background by hand or machine appliqué (see pages 43-46).

The Stitches

There are two basic ways to stitch your appliqué in place, either by hand or machine. The hand stitch, called a blind stitch, is the historical method used by master appliquérs over the past centuries—but the machine stitch can also win a ribbon in the 21st century. Machine stitching does provide a variety of stitches, from a simple satin to a fancier buttonhole stitch

Hand Appliqué Stitch

The hand appliqué stitch, called a blind stitch, is timeless! It hides in the appliqué pieces, allowing the appliqué design to come forward in a three-dimensional relief.

The stitch slightly sits on the appliqué piece, so match the color of the thread to the appliqué piece to keep it from showing. If you cannot find a close match, use a darker thread rather than a lighter, as a lighter one will show up more. While you are appliquéing, occasionally check to make sure you are keeping the background fabric blocked flat by spreading it on a flat surface.

The needleturn method uses this stitch, but it has a few other steps. You will find these directions at the end of this section.

Although the blind stitch that we teach is the most common type of appliqué stitch, you can use any type of embroidery or decorative stitch. Some people prefer to stitch from left to right, while others prefer from right to left. Either way is acceptable; experiment and find which direction is more comfortable for you.

You Will Need

- ❖ Thimble to fit middle finger
- ❖ Applique pins
- ❖ Appliqué needle (Sharp, Milliner, Straw, or Between)
- ❖ Lightweight cotton or silk thread
- ❖ Scissors

1 Thread approximately 18" of thread on the needle.

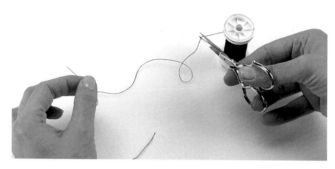

2 Make a knot at the end of the thread where it was cut from the spool. Note: Make a smaller knot with only two loops for tight-weave fabrics, three loops for loose-weaves.

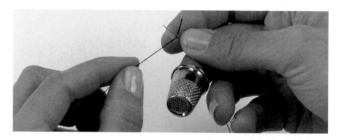

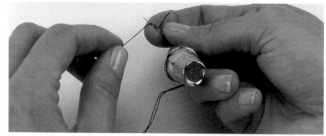

3 Pin an appliqué piece to the background fabric with several small appliqué pins.

4 Hide the knot in the back of the seam allowance of the appliqué piece (not behind the background fabric) by bringing the needle out just on the inside of the seam allowance.

5 Place the needle straight down into the background fabric, directly next to, and perpendicular to where the thread emerged from the appliqué piece. This is the stitch.

6 Bring the needle up approximately 1/16" away through all of the layers, catching about two threads of the appliqué piece. Again, place the needle in the background fabric, perpendicular to where the needle emerged from the appliqué piece, to continue stitching.

(continued on next page)

*B*ecause of the way it is manufactured, thread has a nap. Pulling it through the fabric in the proper direction will prevent it from fraying. To prevent your thread from fraying, knot the end of the thread that was cut from the spool. Try making a "thread library" to store your different threads. The pattern for this handy cloth pouch is made by Lazy Girl Designs.

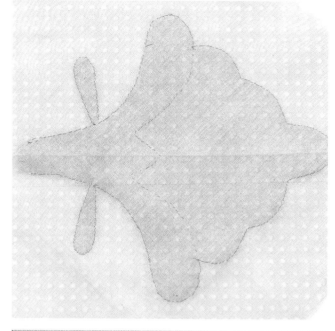

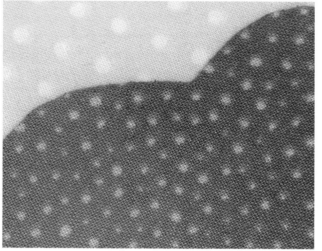

From the front.

From the back.

7 Keep stitches perpendicular, evenly spaced apart, and only catch one or two threads of the appliqué piece to achieve a perfectly hidden appliqué stitch.

8 When you are finished stitching, take the needle to the back and take a small stitch of the background fabric behind the appliqué piece. Make a knot and sink; then slide the needle into the backing behind the appliqué piece, hiding the tail.

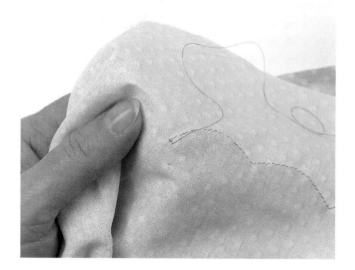

Hand Appliqué Stitch with the Needleturn Method

This stitch is the same as the regular appliqué blind stitch, but here you turn the seam allowance under with the needle just before your stitching line.

1 Secure the appliqué piece to the background fabric with appliqué pins.

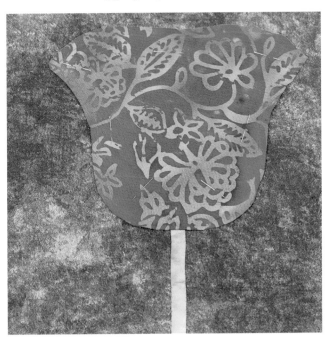

2 Hide the starting knot in the seam allowance of the appliqué piece.

3 Turn under a small amount of the seam allowance, 1/2" or so; with your fingertips, hold in place while you make your first stitch.

4 Make one or two blind stitches, and then tuck more of the seam allowance under with your needle tip.

5 Continue in this manner, tucking under the seam allowance and then taking as many blind stitches as possible.

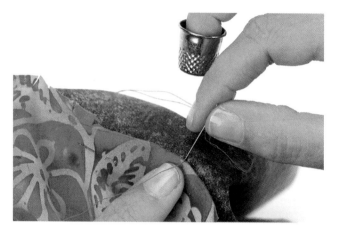

6 When needleturning outward curves or circles, turn under only a small amount of seam allowance and only take two or three stitches at a time. The secret to smooth curves is taking the time to fan out the seam margin underneath with your needle before taking the stitches.

7 For points, appliqué to the end and have your last stitch be "one stitch away from the point." Bring your needle out on the point. Take the stitch, turn under the tip, and trim away the tip of the seam allowance that you turned from under the piece. Turn under the rest of the seam allowance. Tug the thread outward to pull out the point, and then continue down the other side. For very sharp points, you may need to trim the seam margin for it to fit under the point.

8 For an inward "V" shape, make your stitches very close together when working toward the "V" and when working back out the other side. At the "V," where there is no more seam allowance, make the stitches deeper, catching three or four threads of fabric instead of just two threads. The stitch directly in the "V" will be the longest stitch.

Gail and Cindy both stitch from left to right, but many master appliquers stitch from right to left. Try both directions and see which is more comfortable for you.

Machine Appliqué Stitch

Machine appliqué is very popular, because you can use a variety of threads and stitches. Try different decorative stitches, including blanket, feather, and other "fun" stitches. A tight zigzag stitch, called a satin stitch, is easily made with any machine that zigzags, or with a zigzag foot. Machine appliqué the pieces to the background squares before attaching all the squares together.

You Will Need

❖ Machine in good working order with zigzag foot and top stitch needle
❖ Medium-weight cotton thread
❖ Tear-away, or dissolving, stabilizer

1 Gather your sewing supplies. We prefer a top stitch needle, size 80 or 90. Quilter's gloves will make it easier to grasp the project.

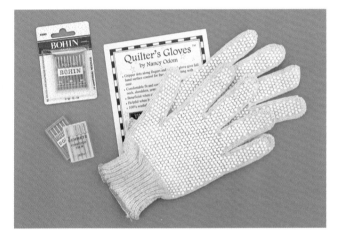

2 Secure the appliqué pieces marked #1 in place either by pinning or applying a spray baste adhesive. Apply a tear-away stabilizer to the wrong side of the background block by either pinning or applying a spray baste adhesive. Some tear-away stabilizers fuse with an iron to the back-side of the background blocks.

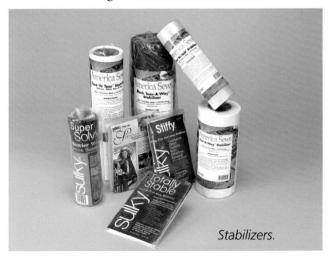

Stabilizers.

3 Use a good quality machine thread. Choose thread colors and a decorative machine stitch that will enhance your appliqué.

4 Set the stitch lengths fairly short, and bring the bobbin thread to the top. Start in an unobvious spot, and stitch all around the appliqué piece.

5 Have fun and don't be afraid to vary the stitches or threads on any one block.

6 Tear away the paper stabilizer from the back.

Turning Your Project Into A Quilt

You are now ready to sew your blocks together to make a quilt top. But, before doing so, you must decide if you would like to add a strip of lattice fabric in between the blocks.

This quilt has no lattice separating the blocks.

Spring Wreath, Mountain Mist pattern #93, 1945, Mrs. H. A. Coulter of Barnville, Ohio. Through the history of quilting, spring flowers have been an important inspiration for designs. Notice how these dainty wreaths form an intriguing design when sewn together on the diagonal. Quilt in the collection of Stearns Technical Textiles, makers of Mountain Mist.

Try adding a lattice between the blocks. We cut this lattice 1-1/2" wide. Blocks and lattice sewn together.

We feel borders are important, and can help pull the colors in the quilt together. We added simple block borders with corner stones, cut 6-1/2" wide.

The next step it to sandwich your quilt.

Two people make the job of sandwiching the quilt layers fast and fun. Here, we are smoothing out the batting. Taping the backing to the table kept it taut.

We prefer holding the layers together with basting spray when machine quilting. Use one of the newer, nontoxic brands such as Sulky's KK2000 or 505

We prefer safety pin basting when hand quilting.

Applique quilts are perfect for either hand or machine quilting. This is a huge topic about which many books are written. Use your preferred method.

If you need a few tips on hand quilting, we recommend *Fine Hand Quilting*, by Cindy Walter and Diana Leone. For machine quilting, we recommend *Machine Quilting Made Easy*, by Maurine Noble.

Binding

Binding a quilt is baffling for some quilters. Here is an easy guide.

Sew 1-1/2" wide, straight-of-grain strips together, creating binding that is longer than the circumference of the quilt. Starting away from a corner, with right side of binding on the top side of the quilt, fold down the raw end of the binding at an angle toward you. When you reach the corner, stop sewing 1/4" from the end.

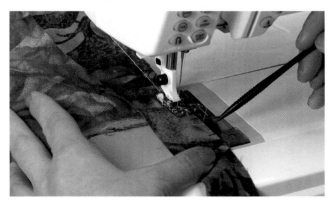

Lift the needle out of the quilt. Rotate the whole quilt. Lift the binding straight up, away from you.

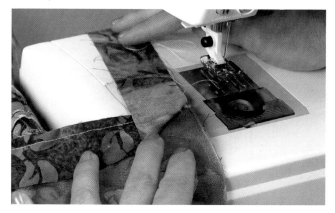

Then fold it toward you.

Start sewing right from the edge. Continue sewing the entire binding in this fashion. When you reach the end of the binding, slightly overlap the starting place.

Working from the back of the quilt, fold half of a width of the binding onto itself.

Then fold once again onto the back of the quilt. Attach using a slipstitch or a blind stitch.

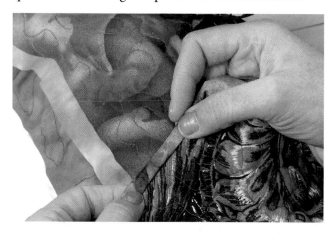

When you reach the corner, stitch up to the seam line, and then turn the second edge once under, and then fold it under again on top of the back, to create a perfect miter.

Section 4
Patterns and Projects

**Project 1
Buds and Leaves**

**Project 2
Triple Tulip**

**Project 3
Tulip Circle**

**Project 4
English Flower Garden Wreath**

**Project 5
Hollyhock Wreath**

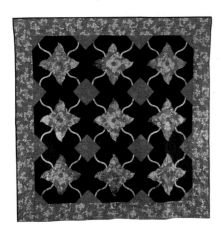

**Project 6
Zinnia**

**Project 7
Rose Cross**

**Project 8
Basket of Posies**

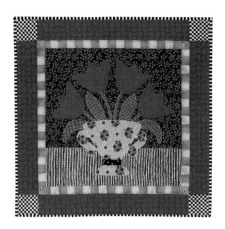

**Project 9
Tulip Vase**

**Project 10
Alice's Basket**

**Project 11
Butterfly**

**Project 12
Lotus Bud**

**Project 13
Iris**

**Project 14
Pansy Wreath**

**Project 15
Ohio Rose**

**Project 16
Indiana Rose**

Buds and Leaves

8" Finished Block

Buds and Leaves, 32" x 40", 2001, by Gail Baker Rowe. Gail used the c.1930 block on the following page as an inspiration for this quilt. She hand-appliquéd the blocks using the needleturn method, and then finished the quilt with hand quilting. The yellow background blocks and the floral-printed border are a perfect setting for this simply darling quilt. This is a wonderful pattern for a beginner and a perfect use for small scraps of fabric.

You Will Need

❖ Fabrics
Background 3/4 yd soft yellow:
  Cut 12 blocks 8-1/2" square
Leaves 1/4 yd green
Buds 36: 3" x 3" of various
  floral-printed scraps
Inner border: 1/4 yd:
  Cut 2: 1-1/2" x 32-1/2"
  Cut 2: 1-1/2" x 26-1/2"
Outer border: 1-1/4 yd:
  Cut 2: 3-1/2" x 34-1/2"
  Cut 2: 3-1/2" x 32-1/2"
❖ Basic appliqué and quilting
  supplies for the methods of
  choice

1 Cut the fabric for the 8" square background blocks.

2 Prepare the bud and leaf pattern pieces and attach to the blocks using your preferred method of appliqué. Pattern pieces on page 120.

3 Arrange the blocks to disperse the color of the buds.

4 Sew three blocks across to make a row; you will be making four rows.

5 Sew the four rows together.

6 Attach the inner border.

7 Attach the outer border.

8 Quilt and bind using your desired method.

Triple Tulip

18" Finished Block

Triple Tulip, 51" x 51", 2002, by Cindy Walter. Cindy selected a printed green fabric on which to set the beautiful tulips. She hand-appliquéd the blocks using the thread basting technique, then machine-quilted the top in a free-motion style.

1 Cut the fabric for the 18-1/2" square background blocks.

2 Prepare the pattern pieces and attach to the blocks using your preferred method of appliqué. Pattern pieces on pages 122 and 123.

3 Sew two blocks across to make a row, adding an 18-1/2" piece of lattice in between them. Repeat for the second row.

4 Sew the two rows together adding a 37-1/2" lattice strip in between them and to the top and the bottom.

5 Sew a 39-1/2" lattice strip to each side of the top.

6 Attach the outer border sewing the shorter borders on first and then the longer.

7 Quilt and bind using your desired method.

Tulip Circle

16" Finished Block

Tuxedo Tulips, 47" x 47", 2001, by Gail Baker Rowe. The formal flare of this Tulip Circle quilt was achieved by adding red fabric on top of black and white batiks. Gail used the needleturn method to appliqué the blocks. It was machine quilted by Cottage Quilting.

1 Cut the fabric for the 16-1/2" square background blocks.

2 Prepare the pattern pieces and attach to the blocks using your preferred method of appliqué. Pattern pieces are on page 124.

3 Sew two blocks across to make a row; you will be making two rows.

4 Sew the two rows together.

5 Attach the inner border, and then the second inner border.

6 Attach the outer border.

7 Quilt and bind using your desired method.

English Flower Garden Wreath

16" Finished Block

English Flower Garden Wreath, 74" x 74", 2001, by Gail Baker Rowe. Gail created this quilt by duplicating the older English Flower Garden quilt featured on page 86. Gail used the needleturn method of appliqué with hand stitching and then hand-quilted the quilt.

You Will Need

❖ Fabrics
Background 2-1/2 yd off white:
   Cut 9 blocks 16-1/2" square
Leaves 1/2 yd green
Flowers a large variety of multi-
   colored fabrics
Lattice and inner border 1-1/2 yd
   green:
   Cut 6: 3" x 16-1/2" (lattice)
   Cut 2: 3" x 53-1/2" (lattice)
   Cut 2: 3" x 58-1/2" (inside bor-
   ders)
   Cut 2; 3" x 53-1/2"
Outer border 1-1/4 yd off-white:
   Cut 2: 8-1/2" x 58-1/2"
   Cut 2: 8-1/2" x 74-1/2"
❖ Basic appliqué and quilting
   supplies for the methods of
   choice

1 Cut the fabric for the 16-1/2" square background blocks.

2 Prepare the pattern pieces and attach to the blocks using your preferred method of appliqué. Pattern pieces are on page 125.

3 Arrange the blocks to disperse the color of the fabrics used. Number the blocks 1 to 3 in the top row, 4 to 6 in the middle row, and 7 to 9 in the bottom row.

4 Sew a 3" x 16-1/2" lattice piece to the right side of blocks 1 and 2. Sew blocks 1, 2, and 3 together to make a row. Repeat adding the lattice and sewing the rows together for the middle and bottom rows.

5 Sew a 3" x 53-1/2" lattice across the bottom of the top and middle rows. Sew the rows together. Attach the inside border.

6 Attach the outer border.

7 Quilt and bind using your desired method.

Hollyhock Wreath

16" Finished Block

Hollyhock Wreath, 66" x 82", 2001, by Gail Baker Rowe. Gail mixed and matched blue floral and green fabrics from her "stash" for this quilt. She used her favorite method of appliqué, needleturn, to create this quilt. Machine quilted by Woodland Manor Quilting.

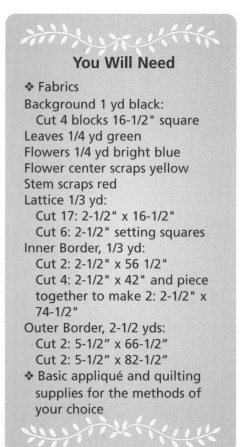

You Will Need

❖ Fabrics
Background 1 yd black:
   Cut 4 blocks 16-1/2" square
Leaves 1/4 yd green
Flowers 1/4 yd bright blue
Flower center scraps yellow
Stem scraps red
Lattice 1/3 yd:
   Cut 17: 2-1/2" x 16-1/2"
   Cut 6: 2-1/2" setting squares
Inner Border, 1/3 yd:
   Cut 2: 2-1/2" x 56 1/2"
   Cut 4: 2-1/2" x 42" and piece
   together to make 2: 2-1/2" x
   74-1/2"
Outer Border, 2-1/2 yds:
   Cut 2: 5-1/2" x 66-1/2"
   Cut 2: 5-1/2" x 82-1/2"
❖ Basic appliqué and quilting
   supplies for the methods of
   your choice

1 Cut the fabric for the 16-1/2" square background blocks.

2 Prepare the pattern pieces and attach to the blocks using your preferred method of appliqué. Pattern pieces are on page 130.

3 Arrange the blocks to disperse the color of the fabrics used. Number the blocks 1 to 3 in the top row, 4 to 6 in the middle rows, and then 10 to 12 in the bottom row.

4 Sew a 3" x 16-1/2" lattice piece to the right side of blocks 1 and 2. Sew blocks 1, 2, and 3 together to make a row.

5 Make three sections of three lattice and setting squares. Attach these between the four rows.

6 Attach the inner border.

7 Attach the outer border.

8 Quilt and bind using your desired method.

Zinnia

14" Finished Block

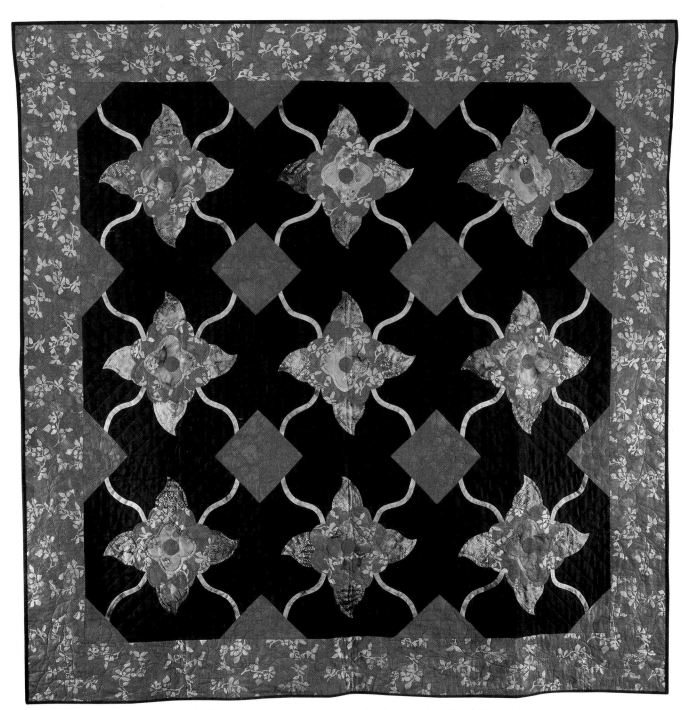

Zinnia, 56" x 56", 2001, by Gail Baker Rowe. By using a black background and bright red batiks, this quilt has an oriental flare. Gail likes using black fabrics, because she feels they enhance the color of the surrounding fabrics. Machine quilted by Woodland Manor Quilting.

You Will Need

❖ Fabrics
Background 2-1/2 yd black:
    Cut 9 blocks 14-1/2" square
Leaves 1/4 yd green
Stems 1/4 yd green
Large flower 1/4 yd bright pink
    floral
Small flower 1/4 yd blue floral
Outer border 1-3/4 yd bright
    pink floral:
    Cut 2: 5-1/2" x 45-1/2"
    Cut 2: 5-1/2" x 55-1/2"
Corner triangles 1/2 yd bright
    pink,
    Cut 4: 4-1/2" square
❖ Basic appliqué and quilting
    supplies for the methods of
    choice

1 Cut the fabric for the 14-1/2" square background blocks.

2 Prepare the pattern pieces and attach to the blocks using your preferred method of appliqué. Pattern pieces are on pages 126 and 127.

3 We used the 4-1/2" squares to create triangles by adding them to the four corners. Place one square on a corner of the background and match edges. Sew across the square diagonally. Fold the square on the sewing line to the corner of the block. Cut away the excess. Press toward the corner.

4 Sew three blocks across to make the rows; you will make three rows.

5 Sew the three rows together.

6 Attach the border.

7 Quilt and bind using your desired method.

Rose Cross

16" Finished Block

Rose Cross, 27" x 62", 2001, by Cindy Walter. Cindy created this wall hanging for a tall, narrow wall in her living room. She used fabrics that she designed For Quilters Only of Springs Industries and the fusible method of appliqué using Steam-A-Seam2 fusible web. This type of quilt could also be used as a table runner.

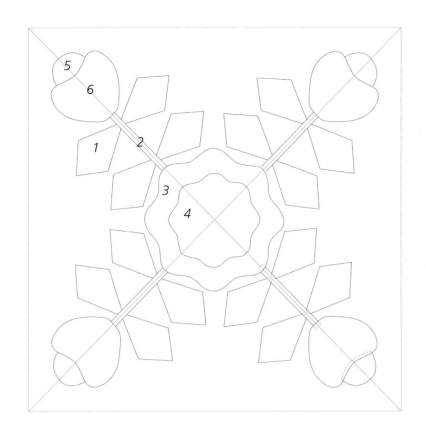

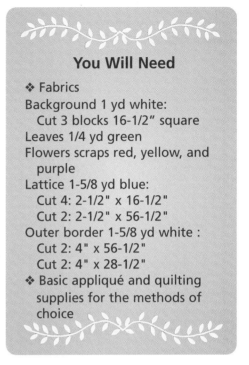

You Will Need

❖ Fabrics
Background 1 yd white:
    Cut 3 blocks 16-1/2" square
Leaves 1/4 yd green
Flowers scraps red, yellow, and
    purple
Lattice 1-5/8 yd blue:
    Cut 4: 2-1/2" x 16-1/2"
    Cut 2: 2-1/2" x 56-1/2"
Outer border 1-5/8 yd white :
    Cut 2: 4" x 56-1/2"
    Cut 2: 4" x 28-1/2"
❖ Basic appliqué and quilting
    supplies for the methods of
    choice

1 Cut the fabric for the 16-1/2" square background blocks.

2 Prepare the pattern pieces and attach to the blocks using your preferred method of appliqué. Pattern pieces are on pages 128 and 129.

3 Sewing a lattice strip between the blocks, sew the three blocks together to make a long row.

4 Sew a lattice strip at each end of the row. Sew a long lattice strip to each side of the long row of blocks.

5 Attach the outer border by sewing a long strip on each side and then sewing the smaller strip to the top and bottom.

6 Quilt and bind using your desired method.

Basket of Posies

13" Finished Block

Basket of Posies, 68" x 68", 2000, by Gail Baker Rowe and Cindy Walter. The quilt that sealed the deal! This was the second quilt in which Gail began using 1930s patterns with contemporary fabrics. Gail used the needleturn method of appliqué, and Cindy finished the quilt with fine stitches of hand quilting.

1 Cut the fabric for the 13-1/2" square background blocks.

2 Prepare the pattern pieces and attach to the blocks using your preferred method of appliqué. Pattern pieces are on page 131.

3 Arrange the blocks to disperse the color of the fabrics used.

4 Sew the blocks together diagonally by beginning in one corner and adding a large triangle to each side of the first appliqué block. For the second row, add a blank block in between the appliqué blocks and then a large triangle on each end. For the third row, sew blank blocks in between three appliqué blocks and then add a small corner triangle to each end. Repeat the second row steps for the fourth row, and the first row steps for the fifth row. Add a small corner triangle to the top of the first and last row. Sew the rows together to create blocks on the diagonal as pictured to the left.

5 Square up the sides before adding the borders. Attach the inner border.

6 Attach the outer border.

7 Quilt and bind using your desired method.

Tulip Vase

16" Finished Block

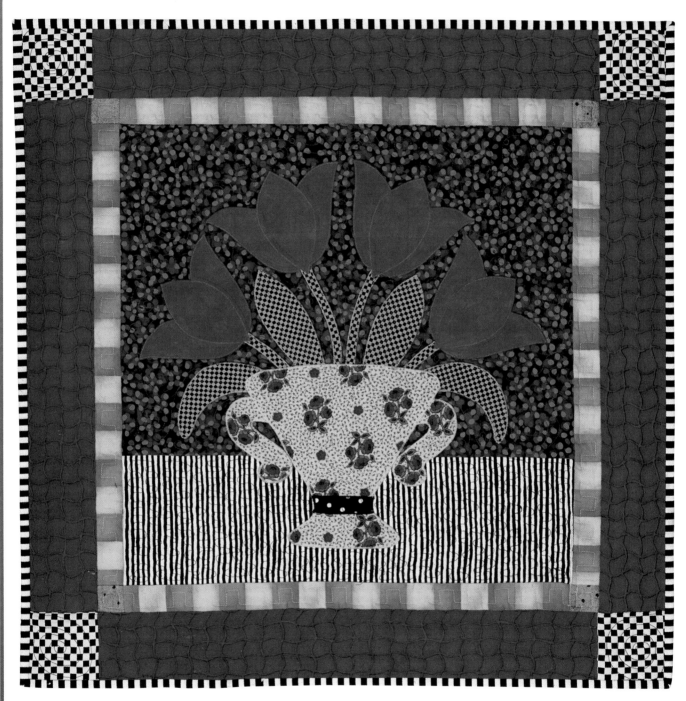

Hot Lips (Tulip Vase), 22" x 22", 2001, by Chris Regina. This wall hanging is a super way to use just one quilt block. Chris' talent for choosing fabric shines in this project. She created her project with fusible web and then finished it by machine appliquéing with a satin stitch.

You Will Need

❖ Fabrics
Background top blue print:
   Cut 1: 11-1/2" x 16-1/2"
Block bottom gray print:
   Cut 1: 5-1/2" x 16-1/2"
Vase 8" x 8" yellow print
Leaves 8" x 8" green
Flowers 8" x 8" red
Inner border 1/4 yd stripes:
   Cut 2: 1" x 16-1/2"
   Cut 2: 1" x 17-1/2"
Outer border 1-1/4 yd red:
   Cut 4: 2-1/2" x 17-1/2"
Border corners scrap gray:
   Cut 4: 2-1/2" x 2-1/2"
❖ Basic appliqué and quilting
   supplies for the methods of
   choice

1 Cut the fabrics for the background block. Sew the gray "tablecloth" to the bottom of the blue printed fabric.

2 Prepare the pattern pieces and attach to the block using your preferred method of appliqué. Pattern pieces are on pages 132 and 133.

3 Attach the inner border.

4 Attach the outer border.

5 Quilt and bind using your desired method.

Alice's Basket

12" Finished Block

Amy's Amish Baskets (Alice's Basket), 58" x 77", 2001, by Susan Colwell. Susan machine-appliquéd this beautiful quilt using both buttonhole and zigzag stitches. She finished off the project by machine quilting using Warm n' Natural batting.

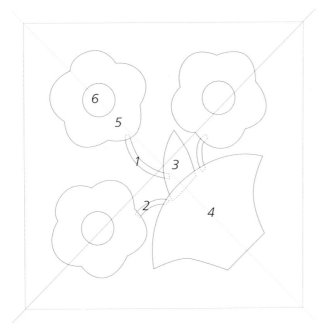

You Will Need

❖ Fabrics
Background 3 yd black:
    Cut 8 blocks 12-1/2" square
    (yardage is for blocks and bor-
    ders)
    Side triangles black:
    Cut 2 blocks 18-1/2" square,
    cut diagonally twice
Corner triangles black:
    Cut 2 blocks 10" square, cut
    diagonally once
Vase 1/4 yd brown
Leaves and stems scraps green
Flowers scraps, variety of colors
Lattice 1 yd blue:
    Cut 12: 1-1/2" x 12-1/2"
    Cut 2: 1-1/2" x 14-1/2"
    Cut 3 1-1/2" x 40-1/2"
Inner border black:
    Cut 2: 2-1/2" x 58-1/2"
    Cut 2: 2-1/2" x 40"
Middle Border 2 yd multi-print:
    Cut 2: 5" x 58"
    Cut 2: 5" x 40"
Outer border black:
    Cut 2: 2-1/2"x 58"
    Cut 2: 2-1/2" x 40"
Corner stones black:
    Cut 4: 9" x 9"
❖ Basic appliqué and quilting
    supplies for the methods of
    choice

1 Cut the fabric for the 12-1/2" square back-ground blocks.

2 Prepare the pattern pieces and attach to the blocks using your preferred method of appliqué. Pattern pieces are on pages 134 and 135.

3 Arrange the blocks to disperse the color of the fabrics used.

4 Sew the short lattice pieces to the top of every block. Sew a short lattice to the other side of two blocks, and sew a 14-1/2" lattice to the ends. With the remaining six blocks, sew three of the blocks together making a row, and then sew one more short lattice to the bottom of the row. Repeat and make a second row.

5 Sew the blocks together to create rows. Follow the photo to the left, adding the large and small triangles where needed.

6 Attach the inner border.

7 Sew a black border strip to each side of a printed strip.

8 Attach the two side borders. Attach the cor-nerstones to the top and bottom borders; then sew them to the quilt.

9 Quilt and bind using your desired method.

Butterfly

9" Finished Block

Butterfly, 34" x 34", 2001, Betty Jane Cheeseman. After finding the blocks that her father had made at her niece's house, Betty sewed them together in 2001. She also made this darling wall hanging by creating nine new blocks.

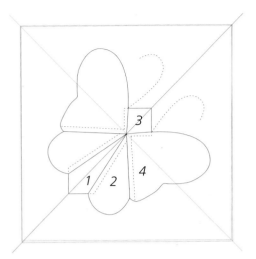

You Will Need

❖ **Fabrics**
Background 1/2 yd white:
  Cut 9 blocks 9-1/2" square
Butterflies 9 scraps of different
  prints
Lattice 1/2 yd purple:
  Cut 6: 2-1/2" x 8-1/2"
  Cut 4: 1/2" x 28-1/2"
  Cut 2: 2-1/2" x 32-1/2"
❖ Basic appliqué and quilting
  supplies for the methods of
  choice

1 Cut the fabric for the 9-1/2" square background blocks.

2 You can treat the butterfly as a single piece or as separate pieces. Prepare the pattern pieces and attach to the blocks using your preferred method of appliqué. Pattern pieces are page 121.

3 Arrange the blocks to disperse the color of the fabrics used.

4 Number the blocks 1 to 3 in the top row, 4 to 6 in the middle row, and 7 to 9 in the bottom row.

5 Sew a 2-1/2" x 8-1/2" lattice piece to the right side of blocks 1, 2, 4, 5, 7 and 8. Sew blocks 1, 2, and 3 together to make a row. Repeat with the next two rows.

6 Sew a 2-1/2" x 28-1/2" piece of lattice between each row and across the top and bottom.

7 Sew a 2-1/2" x 32-1/2" piece of lattice on each side.

8 Quilt and bind using your desired method.

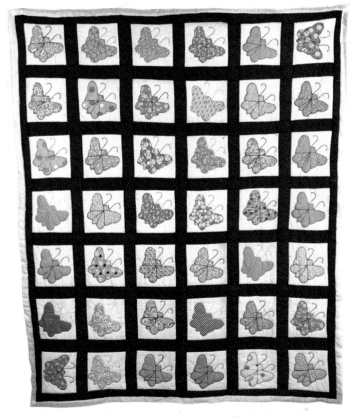

Butterfly, 65" x 73-1/2", 1931 Glen H. Mack. Betty Jane's father, Glen, hand-appliquéd these blocks with a buttonhole stitch. He created the blocks as therapy while he was recovering from tuberculosis at the Oakdale Sanatorium in 1931.

Lotus Bud

16" Finished Block

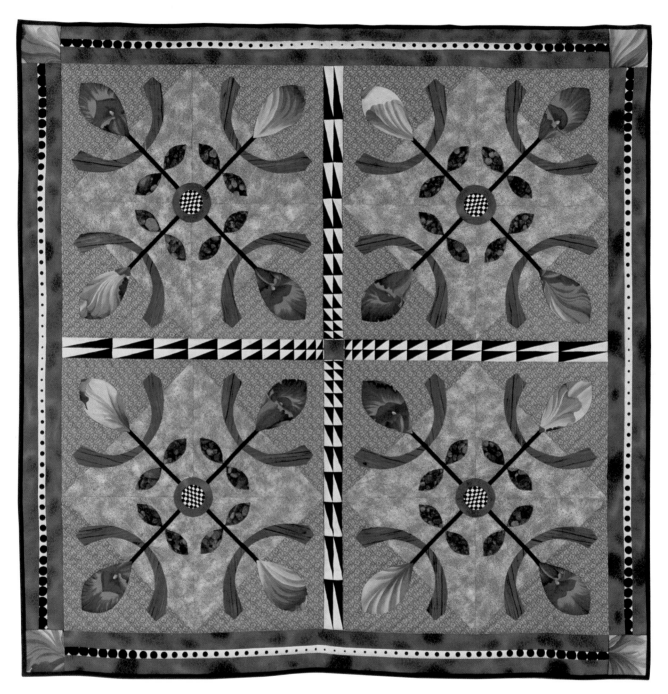

This Bud's for You (Lotus Bud), 38" x 38", 2001, by Barbara Shiffler. This traditional appliqué pattern takes on a new life with the use of contemporary fabrics. Barbara hand-appliquéd the blocks using the freezer paper on the inside method, then finished the quilt with beautiful hand quilting stitches. The background fabrics were a little bright for her taste, so she dulled them by tea dyeing. Even though our directions are for a 16" block, notice that Barbara pieced hers with triangles in the corners. Also, our directions do not piece the lattice or borders, but we encourage you to experiment with different piecing styles, as shown in Barbara's quilt.

You Will Need

❖ Fabrics
Background 1 yd print:
  Cut 4 blocks 16-1/2" square
Leaves 1/8 yd green
Leaves 1/8 yd blue
Flowers 1/8 yd rust
Lattice 1/4 yd multi-print:
  Cut 4: 1-1/2" x 16-1/2"
Lattice center scrap blue:
  Cut 1: 1-1/2" x 1-1/2"
Outer border 1/4 yd multi-print:
  Cut 4: 3" x 33-1/2"
Border corners orange scraps:
  Cut 4: 3" x 3"
❖ Basic appliqué and quilting
  supplies for the methods of
  choice

1 Cut the fabric for the 16-1/2" square background blocks.

2 Prepare the pattern pieces and attach to the blocks using your preferred method of appliqué. Pattern pieces are on page 136.

3 Sew a lattice strip between two blocks. Then sew these together to make the top row. Repeat for the bottom row.

4 Sew the 1-1/2" lattice center square between the remaining two lattices. Carefully match the center seams and sew the lattice strip between the rows of blocks.

5 Attach the outer border by sewing two strips to the sides. Add the border cornerstones to the remaining border strips and sew them onto the top and bottom.

6 Quilt and bind using your desired method.

Iris

12" Finished Block

When Iris Eyes Are Smiling (Iris), 31" x 31", 2001, by Lynda Kepler. What a beautiful setting for this wonderful pattern. Notice how Lynda rotated the four blocks around, creating an "X" pattern with the irises. She used the fusible web method of appliqué and, instead of making bias bars, she used Clover Fusible Bias Tape for the stems. What a great idea!

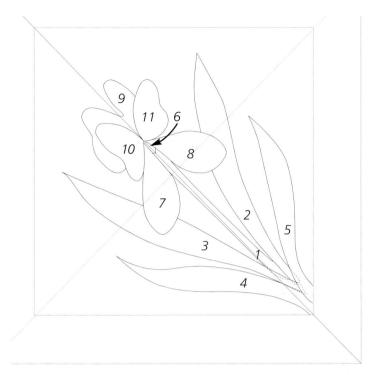

You Will Need

❖ Fabrics
Background 3/4 yd cream:
    Cut 4 blocks 12-1/2" square
Leaves 1/8" green
Flowers scraps of 9 colors
Inner border 1/8 yd gold:
    Cut 2: 1" x 24-1/2"
    Cut 2: 1" x 25-1/2"
Outer border 1/4 yd purple:
    Cut 2: 3-1/2" x 25-1/2"
    Cut 2: 3-1/2" x 31-1/2"
❖ Basic appliqué and quilting
    supplies for the methods of
    choice

1 Cut the fabric for the 12-1/2" square background block.

2 Prepare the pattern pieces and attach to the block using your preferred method of appliqué. Pattern pieces are on pages 138 and 139.

3 Our instructions are for a solid background block. Try experimenting with pieced blocks like the ones in the quilt to the left.

4 Attach the four blocks together to make the inner border.

5 Attach the outer border.

6 Quilt and bind using your desired method.

Pansy Wreath

16" Finished Block

Ring Around the Posey (Pansy Wreath), 40" x 40", 2001, by Linda S. Hoffmeister. Linda used batiks and her own hand-dyed fabrics to create these pansies, which remind her of her colorful garden. She displayed pansies on her design wall and in a bowl by her sewing chair for inspiration. Steam-A-Seam2 was used for the fusible method of appliqué, and she used a machine appliqué stitch. Linda finished the quilt with free-motion machine quilting.

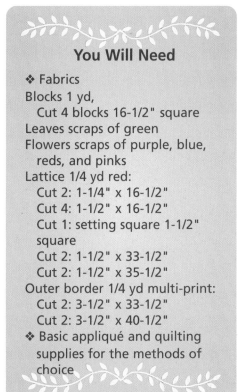

You Will Need

❖ Fabrics
Blocks 1 yd,
    Cut 4 blocks 16-1/2" square
Leaves scraps of green
Flowers scraps of purple, blue,
    reds, and pinks
Lattice 1/4 yd red:
    Cut 2: 1-1/4" x 16-1/2"
    Cut 4: 1-1/2" x 16-1/2"
    Cut 1: setting square 1-1/2"
    square
    Cut 2: 1-1/2" x 33-1/2"
    Cut 2: 1-1/2" x 35-1/2"
Outer border 1/4 yd multi-print:
    Cut 2: 3-1/2" x 33-1/2"
    Cut 2: 3-1/2" x 40-1/2"
❖ Basic appliqué and quilting
    supplies for the methods of
    choice

1 Cut the fabric for the 16-1/2" square background blocks.

2 Prepare the pattern pieces and attach to the blocks using your preferred method of appliqué. Pattern pieces are page 137.

3 Arrange the blocks to disperse the color of the fabrics used.

4 Sew two blocks across to make a row, adding lattice an 16-1/2" piece of lattice in between them. Repeat for the second row.

5 Sew the two rows together adding a 32-1/2" lattice strip in between them and to the top and the bottom.

6 Sew a 34-1/2" lattice strip to each side of the top.

7 Attach the outer border.

8 Quilt and bind using your desired method.

Ohio Rose

16" Finished Block

Ohio Rose, 40" x 50", 2002, by Maureen Shaffer. This talented artist decorated her quilt with several types of embellishments. The ribbon buds and ultra-suede calyxes are an adaptation of a technique learned from Faye Labanaris. The centers of the roses are hand-beaded with seed beads in a variety of colors.

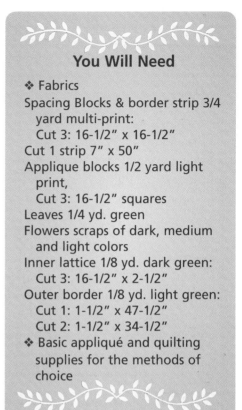

You Will Need

❖ Fabrics
Spacing Blocks & border strip 3/4
    yard multi-print:
    Cut 3: 16-1/2" x 16-1/2"
Cut 1 strip 7" x 50"
Applique blocks 1/2 yard light
    print,
    Cut 3: 16-1/2" squares
Leaves 1/4 yd. green
Flowers scraps of dark, medium
    and light colors
Inner lattice 1/8 yd. dark green:
    Cut 3: 16-1/2" x 2-1/2"
Outer border 1/8 yd. light green:
    Cut 1: 1-1/2" x 47-1/2"
    Cut 2: 1-1/2" x 34-1/2"
❖ Basic appliqué and quilting
    supplies for the methods of
    choice

1 Cut the fabric for the 16-1/2" square background blocks.

2 Prepare the pattern pieces and attach to the blocks using your preferred method of appliqué. Pattern pieces are on pages 140 and 141.

3 Sew a dark lattice strip on one side of each of the three appliqué blocks.

4 Following the photo to the left, sew the appliqué block to a blank block.

5 Staggering which side the blank and appliqué block are on, sew the three rows together.

6 Attach the light green outer border on the left hand side, then attach the light green border to the top and the bottom.

7 Attach the 7" printed border strip to the right hand side.

8 Quilt and bind using your desired method.

Indiana Rose

16" Finished Block

Madras Rose (Indiana Rose), 29" x 29", 2001, by Jane Cole. Jane created the blocks using Heat n' Bond Lite and the fusible appliqué method. She used a combination of unusual fabrics, including batiks, madras plaids, and lamé, which give the quilt texture. For fun, she tipped the center by trimming the borders, rather than leaving them straight.

You Will Need

❖ Fabrics
Block 1 yd gray print:
   Cut 1 block 16-1/2" square
Corner triangle gray print:
   Cut 2 blocks 13-1/2" square,
   cut these in half diagonally
   once
Leaves scraps of green
Flowers 1/2 yd plaids
Center flower scrap red
Lattice 1/4 yd red,
   Cut 2: 1-1/2" x 16-1/2"
   Cut 2: 1-1/2" x 18-1/2"
Border red
   Cut 2: 4" x 25"
   Cut 2: 4" x 33"
❖ Basic appliqué and quilting
   supplies for the methods of
   choice

1 Cut the fabric for the 16-1/2" square background block, and the four triangles.

2 Prepare the pattern pieces and attach to the block using your preferred method of appliqué. Notice one flower petal is added to each corner triangle. Pattern pieces are on page 142.

3 Add the two shorts lattice strips to the side of the block and the two longer ones to the top and bottom.

4 Add the four side triangles; trim if needed to square up the quilt.

5 Attach the outer border by adding the two shorter pieces to the sides and the longer ones on the top and bottom.

6 Quilt and bind using your desired method.

Jane Cole achieved an unusual setting by tilting the block and moving her 6" x 24" inch ruler at an angle, then trimming off the excess border. (See quilt block on page 82.)

Gallery

Tulip Circle, 72" x 72", 2001, by Gail Baker Rowe and Margaret Miller. Gail appliquéd the blocks using the needle-turn method, and world-famous quilter Margaret Miller set the blocks in this exciting fashion using ideas from her latest book, Smashing Sets: Exciting Ways to Arrange Quilt Blocks. Kathy Sandbach machine-quilted this spectacular quilt. Refer to Project 3 for the appliqué pattern.

Tulip Circle, 55" x 41", 2002, by Cindy Walter. Cindy originally made this quilt for an episode of the television show America Sews. Because she used black background blocks, she used black batting; white batting may have bearded onto the black fabric. Refer to Project 3 for the appliqué pattern.

English Flower Garden Wreath, 75" x 77", c.1930, maker unknown. Gail purchased this quilt in 1997 in a small New Hampshire town. It is hand-appliquéd and hand-quilted. Although beautiful, the quilt wasn't in good shape. While mending the quilt, Gail was inspired to reproduce it in today's fabrics; this quilt was the inspiration for the concept of this book. In the private collection of Gail Baker Rowe. Refer to Project 4 for the appliqué pattern.

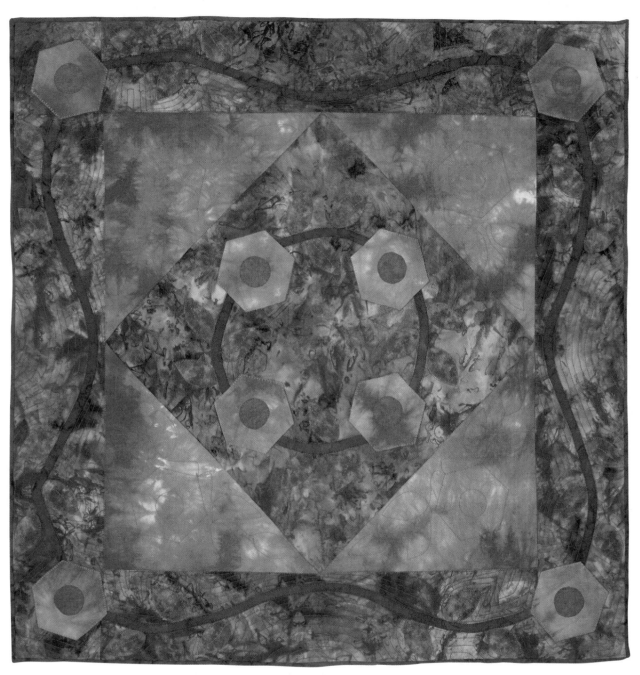

English Flower Garden Wreath, 32" x 32", 2001, by Diana Morrison. Diana created this quilt using Steam-A-Seam2 and the fusible web method of appliqué. She then traced the pattern pieces with a machine blanket stitch. Setting the block on-point added interest to this beautiful quilt. Machine quilted by Eileen Merrick. Refer to Project 4 for the appliqué pattern.

Hollyhock Wreath, 40" x 40", 2001, by Cindy Walter. Cindy created this quilt to use as a demonstration for the PBS television show America Sews. The floral border print offsets the bold black fabric, which is the background. The appliqué was created using the fusible web method and Lite Steam-A-Seam2. Cindy machine quilted this piece. Refer to Project 5 for the appliqué pattern.

Zinnia, 37" x 37", 2001, by Nancy Lee Chong. Nancy is a quilting instructor and designer, specializing in miniature quilts and Hawaiian appliqué. She used the needleturn method of appliqué with size 11 Milliner/Straw needles. For a challenge, she reduced this pattern from a 16" block to 5-1/2". Nancy was especially surprised by the secondary design created by the attaching stems. Refer to Project 6 for the appliqué pattern.

Pienza Sunset (Rose Cross), 45" x 45", 2001, by Judy Kearns. This is another variation on how to arrange the Rose Cross blocks. A trip to Tuscany inspired the colors for this quilt. The swag design on the border is in memory of the flower-filled terra cotta pots of Italy. This quilt was appliquéd with the freezer paper method and machine appliquéd and quilted. The books of master appliquér Elly Sienkiewicz always inspire Judy. Refer to Project 7 for the appliqué pattern.

Basket of Posies, 38" x 38", 2001, by Linda West. Linda used mostly fabric pieces from her scrap bag for this darling quilt. She used the freezer paper needleturn appliqué method with #10 milliner needles. She finished the piece with hand quilting. Refer to Project 8 for the appliqué pattern.

Batik Tulips, 58" x 58", 2002, by Gail Baker Rowe. Gail really enjoyed working on this quilt using the Tulip Vase pattern and her stash of batik fabrics. The colorful variegated cotton thread enhanced the quilting design. Machine quilted by Cottage Quilting. Refer to Project 9 for the appliqué pattern.

Tulip Vase, 17-1/2" x 17-1/2", c.1930, maker unknown. Gail bought this vintage 1930s block on the Internet, at eBay.com. She used it as the pattern for Batik Tulips. In the private collection of Gail Baker Rowe.

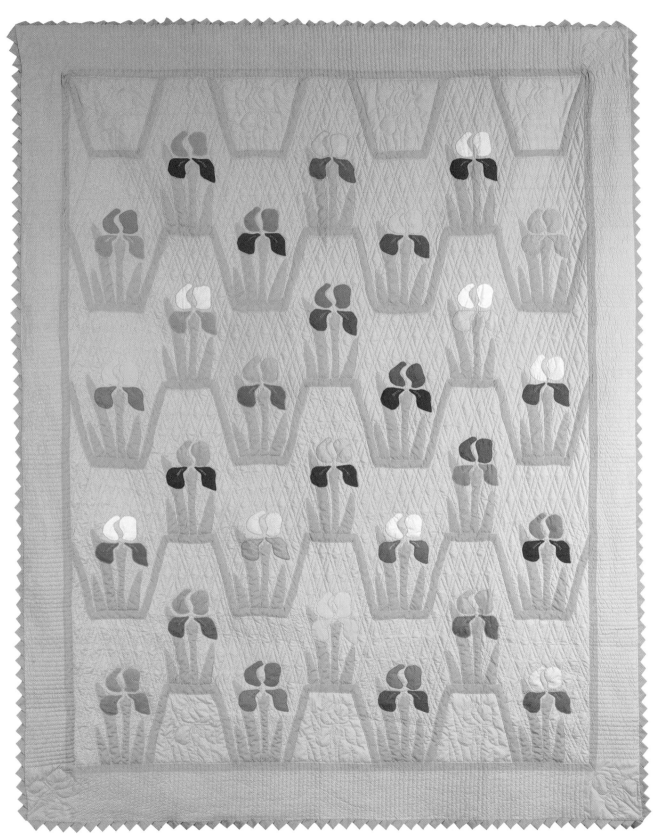

Iris, Mountain Mist pattern # R, 1930, Maker unknown. This historical quilt shows a beautiful way to put the irises in a natural design using actual iris colors. Hand quilted in a grid pattern using Mountain Mist cotton batting. Quilt from the collection of Stearns Technical Textiles, maker of Mountain Mist.

Blazing Tulips (Tulip Circle), 36" x 36", 2001, by Faye Labanaris. A talented quilter, Faye created this interesting wall hanging by setting one Tulip Circle block on the diagonal. Notice her exciting choice of border fabric. She is the author of several books including Quilts with a View *and* Garden View Appliqué. *Refer to Project 3 for the appliqué pattern.*

Wild Rose, 40" x 40", 2001, by Joan H. Butler. Joan was very pleased with the results of her quilt, even though she isn't particularly enamored of the color yellow. Joan learned how to needleturn appliqué in a class taught by author Jeanna Kimball; we recommend her book, Red and Green: An Appliqué Tradition. *Joan's grandmother taught her how to sew and to appreciate handwork; she finished this quilt on what would have been her grandmother's 133rd birthday.*

Wild Rose, 36" x 37", 2001, Mary L. Greven. Mary hand-appliquéd the blocks using the freezer paper "on top" method and size 12 Sharp needles. She finished the wall hanging by hand quilting. As with many special quilts, once Mary finished the quilt, she realized she had twisted the direction of the leaves. We're glad she didn't "fix" them; it is one of the quilt's endearing features.

Rare Old Tulip, 31" x 31", 2002, by Stevii Graves. Stevii used a very interesting chenille fabric in the inner borders. It is available by the inch from Fabric Café (see sources). She created the flowers with fabrics she hand-dyed and used the fusible web method of appliqué. Look at the clever stitches on the flowers; they were added with a permanent fabric pen.

POMEGRANATE – Mountain Mist Pattern #31, ©1932, maker unknown. The Pomegranate, sometimes called "Love Apple" and a fruit of considerable legend down the ages, is treated conventionally as in the New England quilt that inspired it. Cotton batting. Quilt from the collection of Stearns Technical Textiles, maker of Mountain Mist.

Tulip Bouquet, 40" x 40", 2001, by Cindy Walter and Gail Baker Rowe. Jennifer Priestly and her mother, Jane Varcoe, hand-painted the fabrics for this quilt. Gail hand-appliquéd the pieces using the needleturn method, and Cindy finished the piece with free-motion machine quilting. What a great team effort! They created the quilt for Cindy's and Jennifer's book, The Basic Guide to Dyeing & Painting Fabrics.

Hollyhocks, 40" x 40", 2002, by Cindy Walter. Cindy set these beautiful fuchsia-colored flowers on a dark green background, creating a stunning contrast; the jungle-print border fabric is the perfect compliment. Cindy used Lite Steam-A-Seam2, a double-stick lightweight fusible web for quilts and garments. She created this quilt for one of her appearances on the television show America Sews. Refer to Project 5 for the appliqué pattern.

Morning Glory, 49" x 49", 2001, by Nancy Howard. This quilt gives the impression of balance, even though it is set on-point. It is a "double" quilt; the blue quilt is a separate finished quilt. The Morning Glory quilt was layered on top, giving a feeling of depth, and the appliquéd morning glories seem to be framed by a window. The project is finished with hand quilting.

Dancing Dahlias, 32" x 38", 2001, by Billece Morrison. The dahlias dance on this quilt because of their varied sizes. What a beautiful setting for this traditional pattern! The blocks were attached with the fusible web method and Steam-A-Seam2 and then stitched over with a buttonhole stitch. As a side note, Cindy wants you to know that Billece, a native of Louisiana, makes the best jambalaya!

A Rose with a Checkered Past (Carolina Rose), 40" x 40", 2001, by Jane Cole. Notice how Jane first pieced together alternating squares of white and black fabrics to make the background blocks. Then, she appliquéd the pieces using the fusible appliqué method with Heat n' Bond Lite.

Pomegranate Picnic (Pomegranate), 41" x 41", 2001, by Wendy Bowen. The background blocks are pieced with four black and white half-square-triangle squares in each block. What a super background! Wendy then appliquéd the pieces using the fusible appliqué method with Heat n' Bond Lite. Her interesting border treatment adds a wonderful final touch.

May Basket, 52" x 54", 2002, by Cindy Walter and Gail Baker Rowe. Gail hand-appliquéd this stunning quilt top as a gift for Cindy. The baskets are set on the diagonal, and the whole top was tea-dyed to give it a softer look. Cindy finished the quilt with hand quilting.

May Basket, 14-3/4" x 15-1/4", 2002, by Maria Lage. Maria reduced the original 14" block to 4-1/2" and then incorporated it into this miniature medallion-style quilt. Maria, an experienced quilter, used a variety of print sizes to capture the realistic shading in the appliqué pieces. To attach the appliqué pieces she used the freezer paper "on top" with needleturn method.

Purple Party, 44" x 44", 2002, by Deborah Sylvester. Deborah is known for her award-winning quilts. Her talent shines through here with her selection of fabrics for these traditional Hollyhock blocks. She appliquéd the pieces using the fusible appliqué method with Steam-A-Seam2 and finished the quilt with decorative free-motion machine quilting. To view some other of Deborah's beautiful quilts visit her Web site, Sylvesterartquilt.com. Refer to Project 5 for the appliqué pattern.

English Flower Garden, 36" x 36", 2001, by Dorothy Krueger. Dorothy created the blocks with the fusible method and Pellon Wonder Under fusible web. After fusing, she outlined the appliqué pieces using a machine blanket stitch. Pattern available in Worth Doing Twice, *Krause Publications. Dorothy is the owner of the Sew Crazy Shop in Plymouth, Massachusetts.*

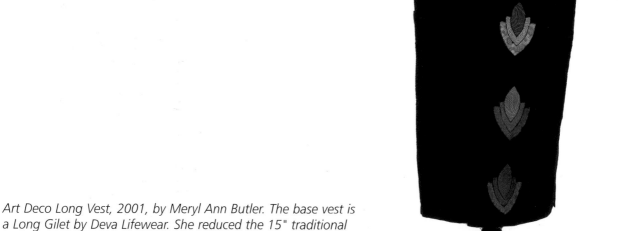

Tuxedo Jacket, 2001, by Meryl Ann Butler. The base garment is a Tuxedo Jacket by Deva Lifewear. She used the tulips from the traditional Tulip and Rose block and the entire Tulip Bouquet block. She reduced both of the 16" patterns by 76 percent. Meryl used Steam-A-Seam2 with the fusible web method of appliqué and 1/4" Clover Quick Bias fusible bias tape in green and dark green.

Art Deco Long Vest, 2001, by Meryl Ann Butler. The base vest is a Long Gilet by Deva Lifewear. She reduced the 15" traditional peonies block by 85 percent. Meryl used Steam-A-Seam2 with the fusible web method of appliqué.

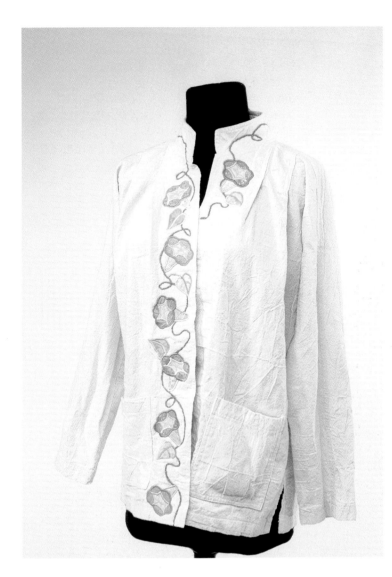

Morning Glory Jacket, 2001, by Meryl Ann Butler. The 100 percent cotton base jacket is a Bolero Jacket by Deva Lifewear. Meryl used Steam-A-Seam2 with the fusible web method of appliqué. To add the couched-on yarns, she suggests to first draw a vine design on the garment with chalk or a water-soluble pen. Couch down the yarn following the line.

Wild Rose Dress, 2001, by Meryl Ann Butler. The jade-colored 100-percent cotton base garment is a Dierdre dress by Deva Lifewear. Meryl used Steam-A-Seam2 with the fusible web method of appliqué and 1/4" Clover Quick Bias fusible bias tape in ivory to create this traditional Wild Rose block. This world-renowned seamstress says to always try on a garment and check the placement of the appliqué motif in relationship to the chest before sewing.

Dutch Tulips, 35" x 60", 2001, by Martine House. The use of batik fabrics and fusible web gives this traditional quilt a very contemporary look. To add complexity to your quilt, follow Martine's example and use several different fabrics of the same color family.

Day Lily, Hawaiian pattern by Elizabeth Root. The Hawaiians use the needleturn method of appliqué and often use only two colors of fabric. You can find this pattern in the book Menehune Quilts…the Hawaiian Way. *View more of Elizabeth's patterns at www.quiltshawaii.com.*

Crowns & Kahili, Hawaiian pattern by Elizabeth Root. The symbols of Hawaiian royalty were often used in the early Hawaiian quilt designs. They use an eight-fold method to cut the pieces and the needleturn method of appliqué. You can find this pattern in the book Menehune Quilts…the Hawaiian Way. *View more of Elizabeth's patterns at www.quiltshawaii.com.*

Martha Washington Wreath, 23" x 46-1/2", 2002, by Gail Baker Rowe. To make this wall quilt more contemporary, Gail added her borders and sashing with a flare. The machine quilting by Cottage Quilting enhances the whimsical border fabric.

Tangerine Trees & Marmalade Skies, 54" x 70", 2002, by Judy Damon. The psychedelic multi-color fabrics used in this quilt remind Judy of 1960s pop art. The title of the quilt is derived from a song by the Beatles, "Lucy in the Sky With Diamonds." Notice how she turned the four center blocks on the diagonal and added several borders. She used an appliqué block pattern called Tangerine. Judy is the owner of the Quiltopia Shop in Hollis, New Hampshire (www.quiltopia.com).

Grandmother Clark and Me, 35-1/4" x 35-1/4", 2001, by Carolyn Slack. *Although we didn't know Grandmother Clark, her tulip design was the inspiration for this quilt using the Rare Old Tulip pattern. Carolyn created this quilt using Steam-A-Seam2 fusible web and a method called "outlining," which uses a donut shape of fusible web to avoid thick layers. Debra Wagner teaches the technique in* Traditional Quilts, Today's Techniques.

Butterflies, Mountain Mist Butterfly pattern #33, 1933, maker unknown. This is an irresistible way to place your butterflies and other designs on a whole-cloth to create a baby quilt. Quilt from the collection of Stearns Technical Textiles, maker of Mountain Mist.

Sources and Suppliers

The Authors

Cindy Walter
C/o Krause Publications
700 East State Street
Iola, WI 54990-0001
snippetsensations@aol.com
www.CindyWalter.com
Internationally known speaker, teacher, quilt designer, and fabric designer. Author of *Snippet Sensations, More Snippet Sensations, Fine Hand Quilting, Attic Windows, Basic Guide to Dyeing & Painting Fabric, Snippet Flower Bouquets, and Snippet Christmas Celebrations.*

Gail Rowe
100 Newton St.
Southboro, MA 01772
rowequilts@aol.com
Quilting teacher, speaker and quilt designer.

Suppliers

Celtic Design Company
834 W. Remington Dr.
Sunnyvale, CA 94087-0643
philomenad@aol.com
Patterns and Celtic Bar

Cottage Quilting
70 Greenwood Ave.
Wakefield, MA 01880
781-245-6906
Quilting services

Deva Lifewear
800-222-8024
www.devalifewear.com
Manufactured base clothing

Fabric Care
12973-C Hwy 155 So.
Tyler, Texas 75703
Chenille fabrics

Fabric Place
136 Howard Street
Framingham, MA 01772
www.fabricplace.com
Fabric and quilting supplies

Fabrics To Dye For
2 River Rd.
Pawcatuck, CT 06379
888-322-1319
www.Fabricstodyefor.com
Wholesale /retail hand-painted fabric and paint/dye supplies

Husqvarna Viking
VSM Sewing Inc.
31000 Viking Pkwy.
Westlake, OH 44145
800-358-0001
Sewing machines

Lazy Girl Designs
437 Maplebrooke Dr. E.
Westerville, OH 43082
614-794-9939
patterns@Lazygirldesigns.com
Purse and pouch patterns

Elizabeth Root
Hawaiian Designing Collection
940 Maunawili Rd.
Kailua, HI 96734
808-261-5151
Quilts@hawaii.rr.com
Hawaiian quilt patterns

Stearns Technical Textiles Co.
100 Williams St.
Cincinnati, OH 45215
800-345-7150
Mountain Mist

The Warm Company
954 E. Union
Seattle, WA 98122
Manufacturers of Steam-A-Seam2 and Warm n' Natural batting

Woodland Manor Quilting
7 Merchant Rd.
Hampton, NH 03844
Quilting services

Notions Supplied

American & Efird, Inc.
Bohin of France
Clover
Coats & Clark
Fairfield Processing
   Corporation
Fiskars, Inc.
Golden Threads
Gingher
Gutermann of America
Hobbs
HTC
Kelsul, Inc.
LYI
Morning Glory
New Cities Designer Fabrics
Northcott/Monarch Fabrics
Olfa Products
Omnigrid
Pellon
Prym-Dritz Corporation
Springs OTC
Sulky of America
W.H. Collins
Wrights

Recommended Reading

Dietrich, Mimi. *Hand Applique*. Bothell, WA: That Patchwork Place, 1998.

Havig, Bettina. *Carrie Hall Blocks*, Paducah, KY: AQS, 1999.

Kimball, Jeanna. *Red and Green: An Applique Tradition*. Bothell, WA: That Patchwork Place, 1990.

Labanaris, Faye. *Garden View Appliqué, Vintage Album Patterns*. Paducah, KY: AQS, 2002.

Labanaris, Faye. *Quilts with a View, A Fabric Adventure*. Paducah, KY: AQS, 1998.

Malone, Maggie. *Treasury of Appliqué Quilt Patterns*. NY: Sterling Publishing Co., Inc., 1995.

Miller, Margaret. *Block Bender Quilts*. Concord, CA: C&T Publishing, 1995.

Miller, Margaret. *Smashing Sets: Exciting Ways to Arrange Quilt Blocks*. Concord, CA: C&T Publishing, 2000.

Morris, Patricia and Jeannette T. Muir. *Worth Doing Twice*. Iola, WI: Krause Publications, 1999.

Noble, Maurine. *Machine Quilting Made Easy*. Bothell, WA: That Patchwork Place, 1994.

Reinstatler, Laura Munson. *Botanical Wreaths, Nature's Glory in Appliqué*. Bothell, WA: That Patchwork Place, 1994.

Root, Elizabeth. *The Pillows to Patch Quilt Collection…the Hawaiian Way*. Kailua, HI: Elizabeth Roots Designs, Inc., 2002.

Root, Elizabeth. *Menehune Quilts…the Hawaiian Way*. Kailua, HI: Elizabeth Roots Designs, Inc., 2001.

Sienkiewicz, Elly. *Baltimore Album Legacy*. Concord, CA: C&T Publishing, 1998.

Sienkiewicz, Elly. *The Best of Baltimore Beauties*. Concord, CA: C&T Publishing, 2000.

Sienkiewicz, Elly. *Fancy Appliqué: 12 Lessons to Enhance Your Skills*. Concord, CA: C&T Publishing, 1999.

Wagner, Debra. *Traditional Quilts, Today's Techniques*. Iola, WI: Krause Publications, 1997.

Waldvogel, Merikay. *Patchwork Souvenirs of the 1933 Chicago World's Fair*. Nashville, TN: Rutledge Hill Press, 1993.

Waldvogel, Merikay. *Quilts of Tennessee: Images of Domestic Life prior to 1930*. Nashville, TN: Rutledge Hill Press, 1998.

Waldvogel, Merikay. *Soft Covers for Hard Times*. Nashville, TN: Rutledge Hill Press, 1990.

Waldvogel, Merikay. *Southern Quilts: Surviving Relics of the Civil War*. Nashville, TN: Rutledge Hill Press, 1998.

Walter, Cindy and Diana Leone. *Attic Windows*. Iola, WI: Krause Publications. 2000.

Walter, Cindy and Diana Leone. *Fine Hand Quilting*. Iola, WI: Krause Publications. 2000.

Walter, Cindy. *More Snippet Sensations*. Iola, WI: Krause Publications, 2000.

Walter, Cindy. *Snippet Sensations*. Iola, WI: Krause Publications, 1996.

Walter, Cindy and Jennifer Priestley. *The Basic Guide to Dyeing & Painting Fabric*. Iola, WI: Krause Publications, 2002.

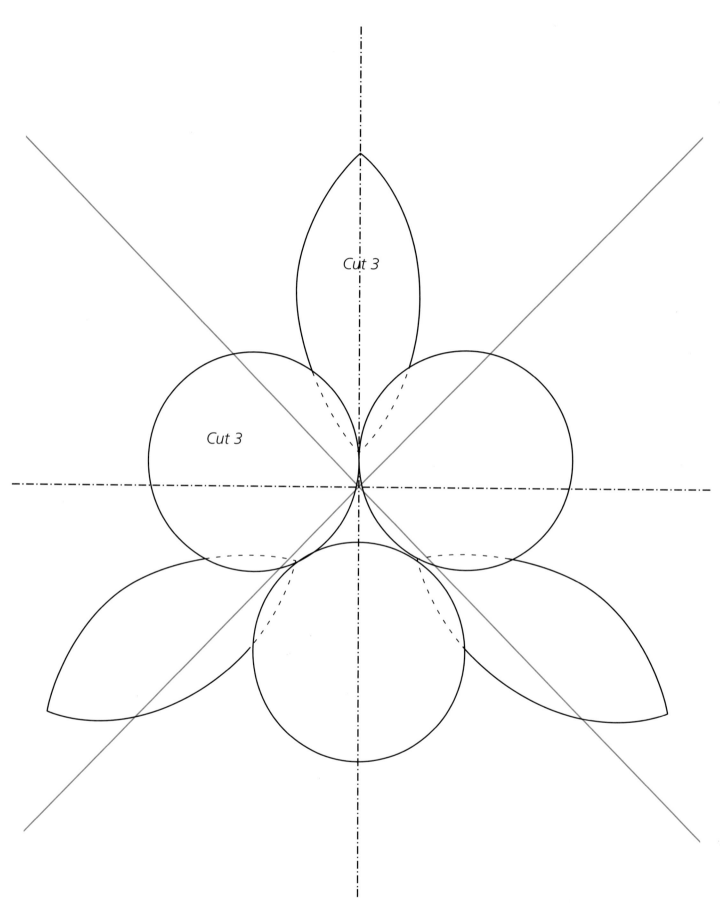

Cut 3

Cut 3

Buds and Leaves Appliqué, Project 1, page 52

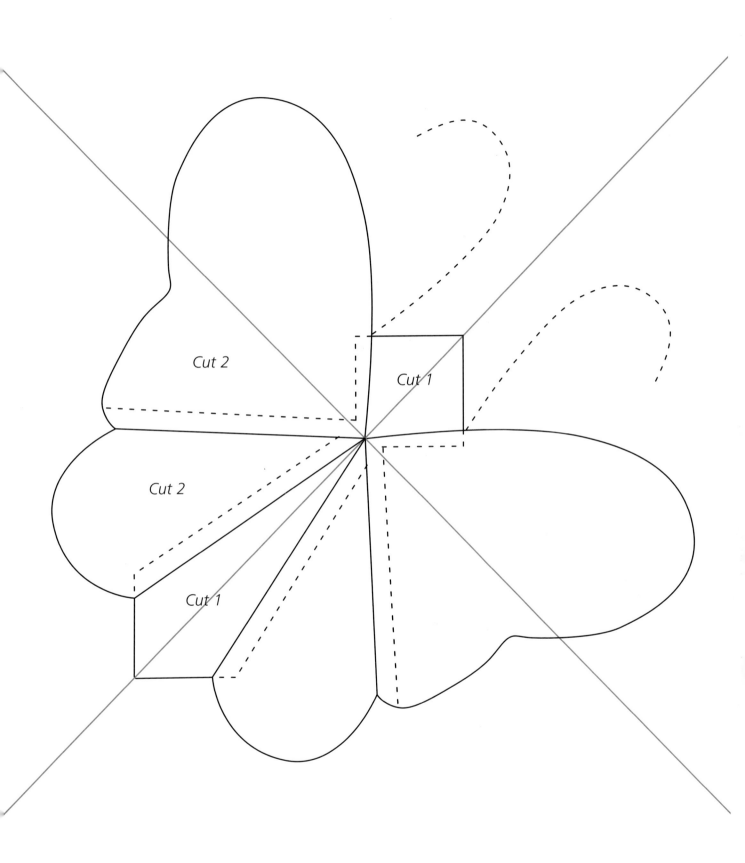

Cut 2

Cut 1

Cut 2

Cut 1

Butterfly Appliqué, Project 11, page 72

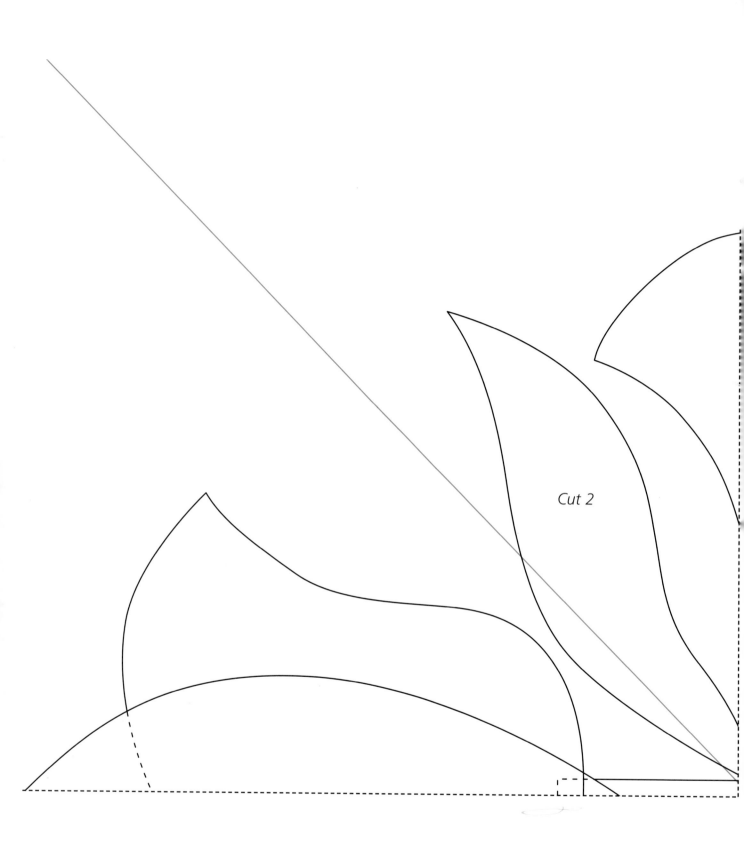

Cut 2

Triple Tulip Appliqué, Project 2, page 54

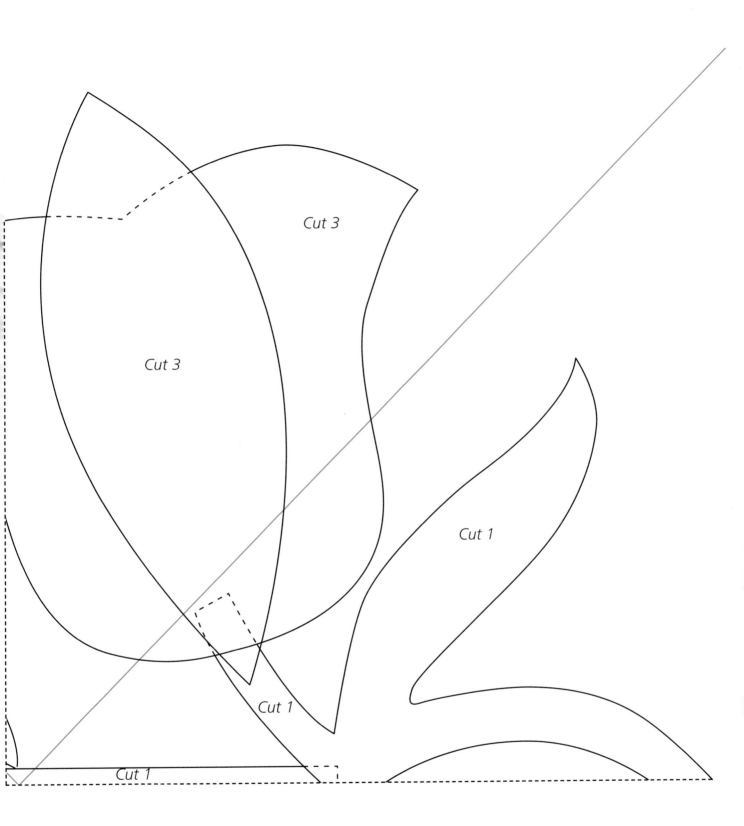

Cut 3

Cut 3

Cut 1

Cut 1

Cut 1

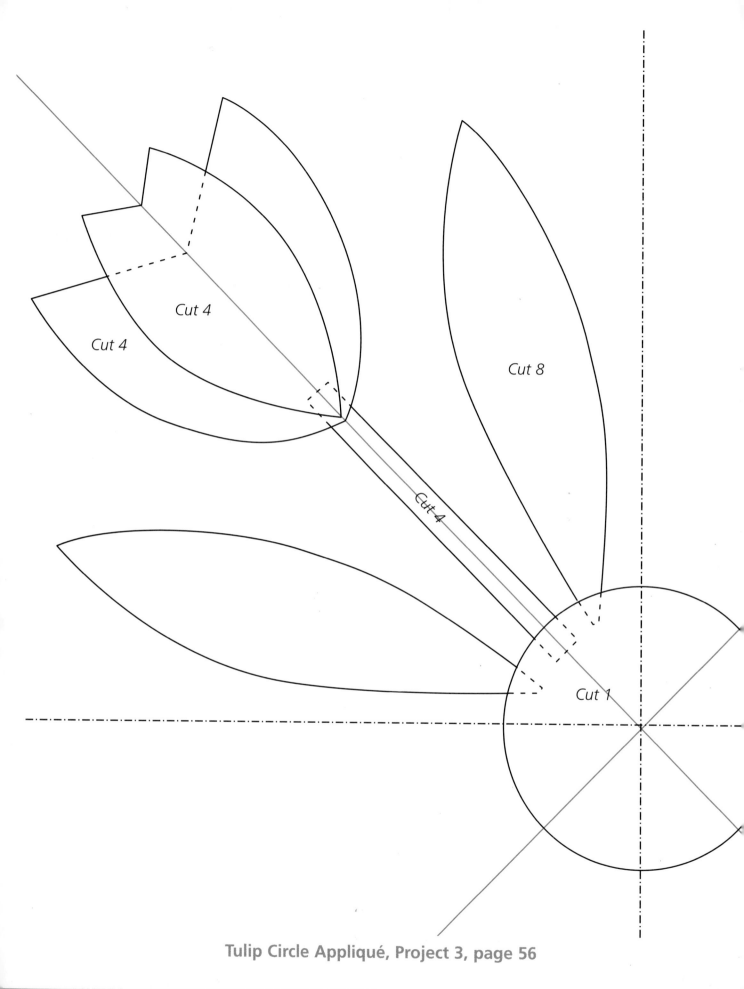

Cut 4

Cut 4

Cut 8

Cut 4

Cut 1

Tulip Circle Appliqué, Project 3, page 56

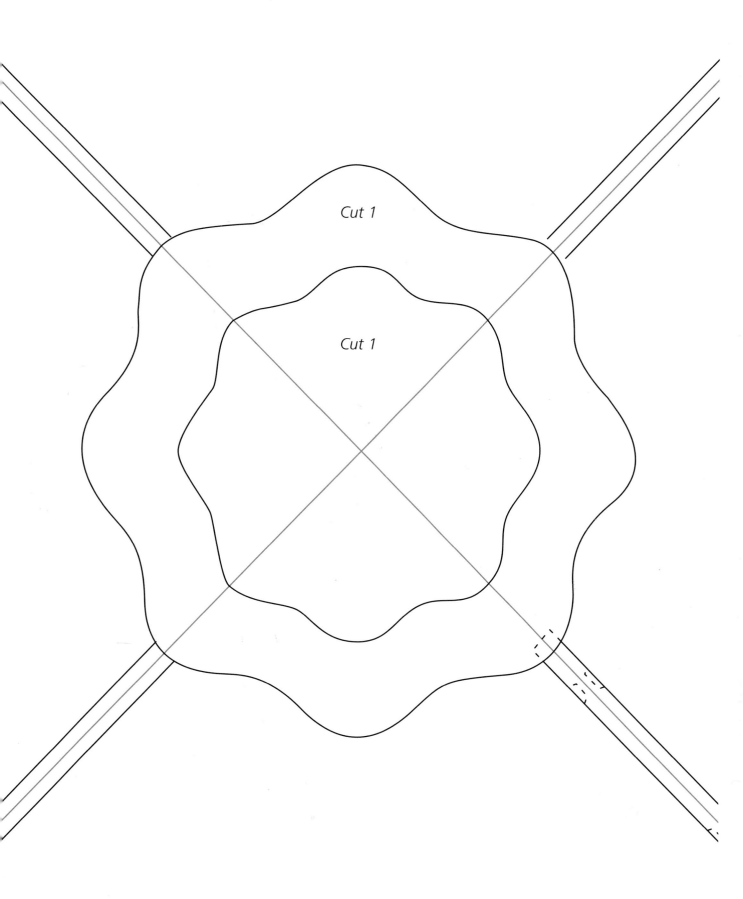

Cut 1

Cut 1

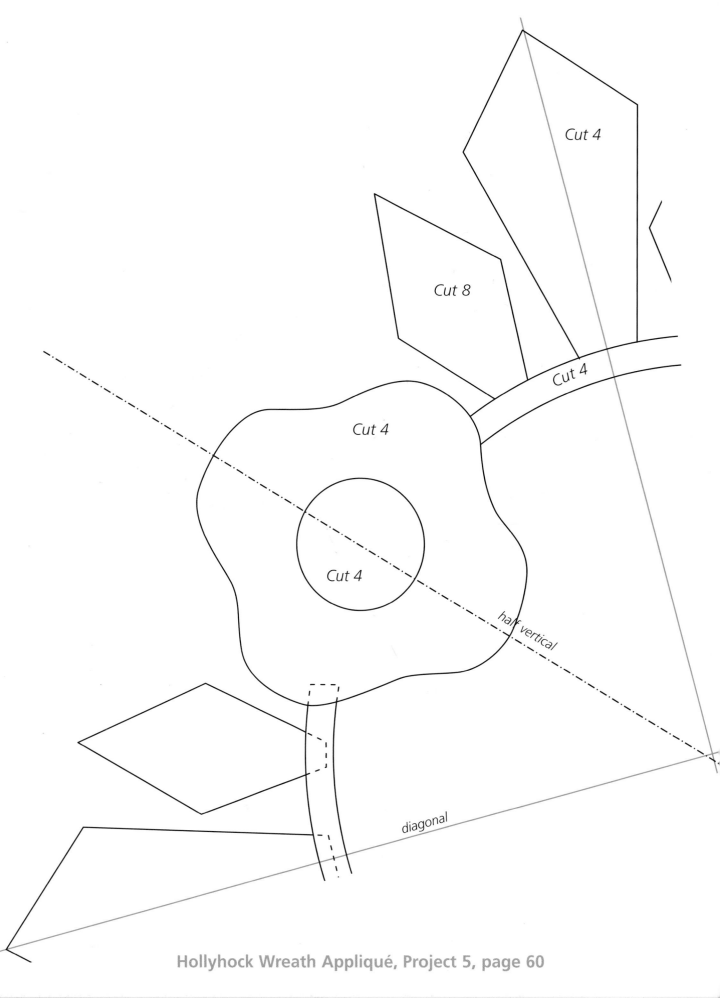

Cut 4

Cut 8

Cut 4

Cut 4

Cut 4

half vertical

diagonal

Hollyhock Wreath Appliqué, Project 5, page 60

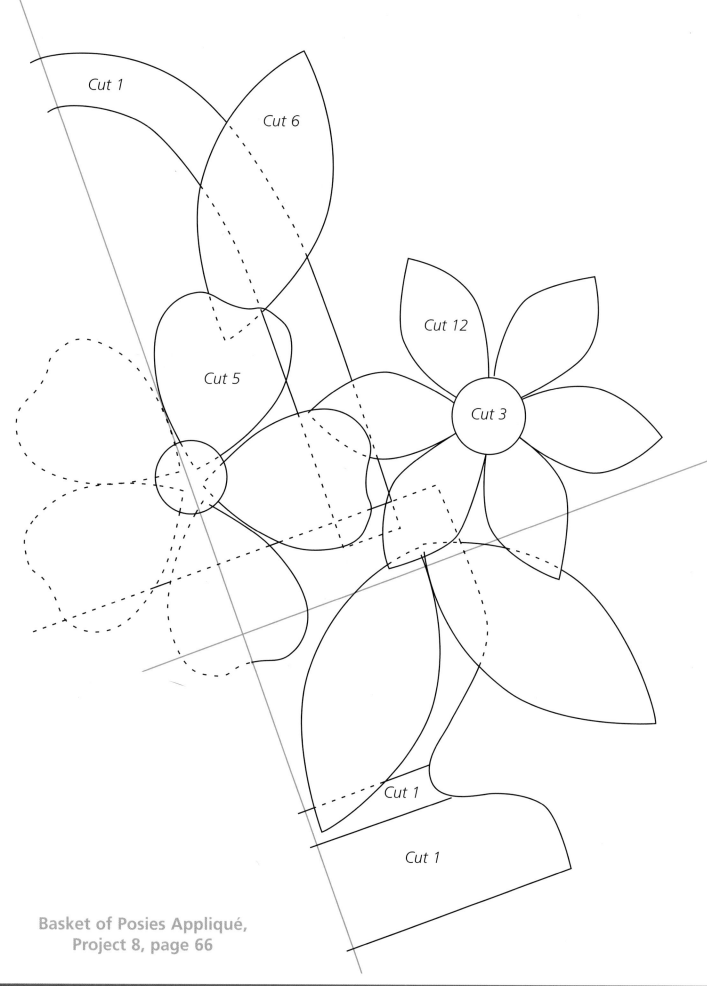

Cut 1

Cut 6

Cut 12

Cut 5

Cut 3

Cut 1

Cut 1

**Basket of Posies Appliqué,
Project 8, page 66**

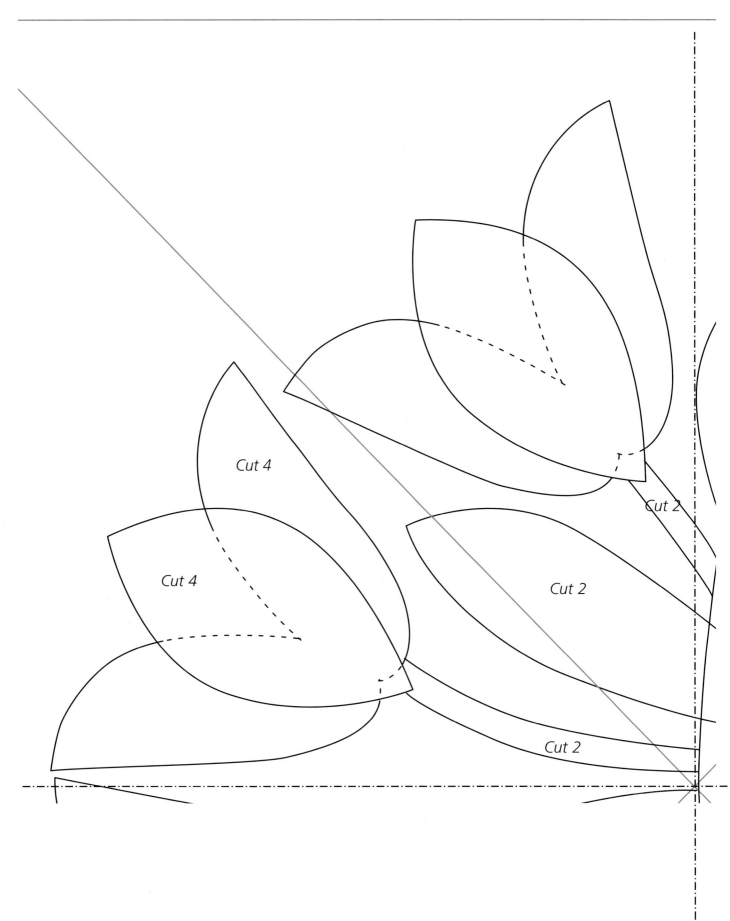

Cut 4

Cut 4

Cut 2

Cut 2

Cut 2

Tulip Vase Appliqué, Project 9, page 68

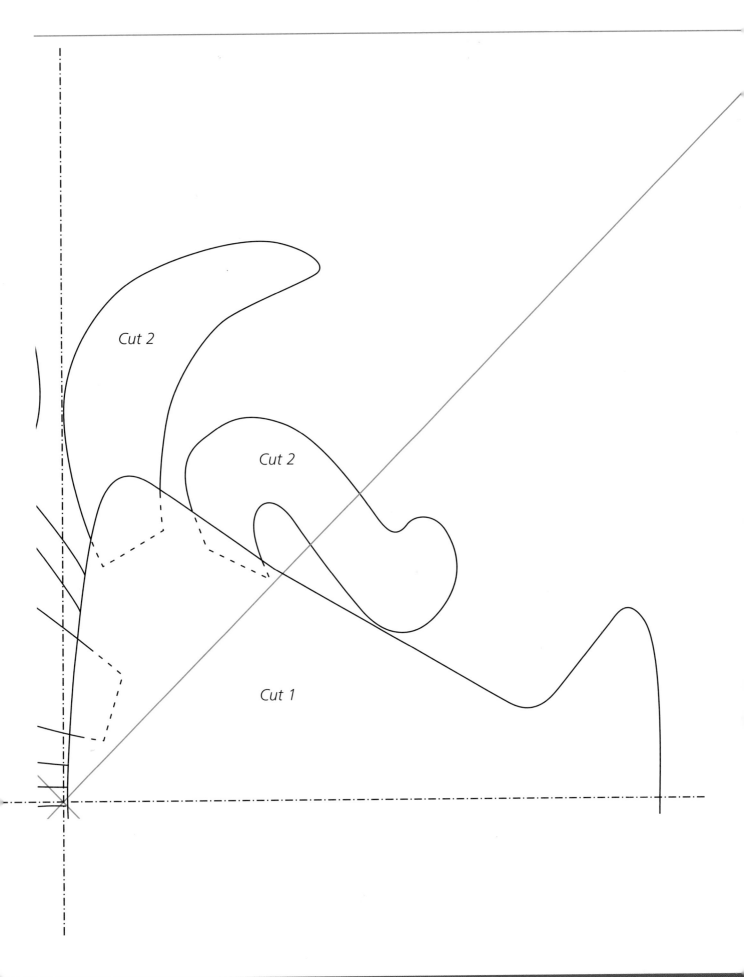

Cut 2

Cut 2

Cut 1

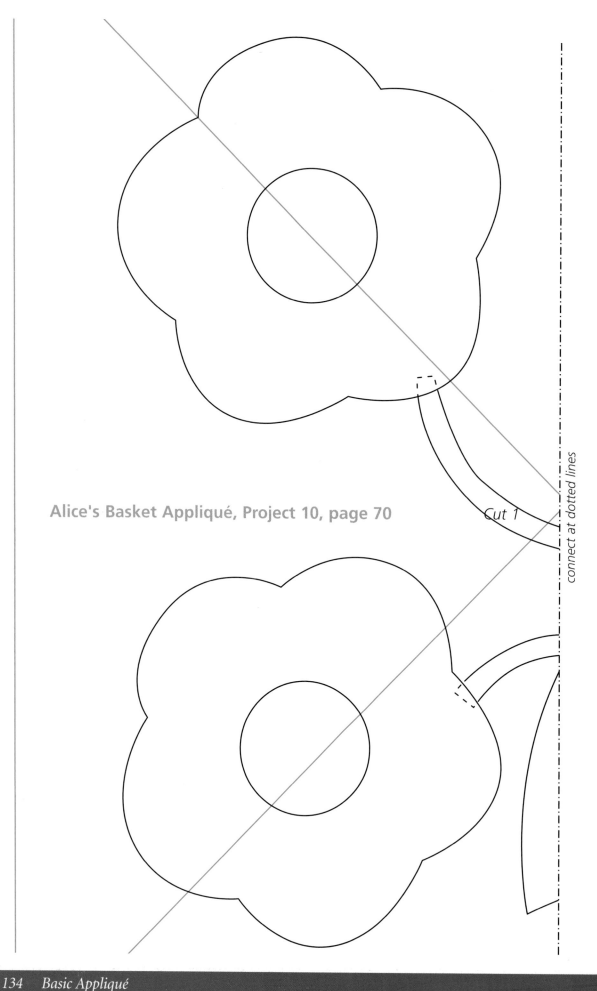

Alice's Basket Appliqué, Project 10, page 70

Cut 1

connect at dotted lines

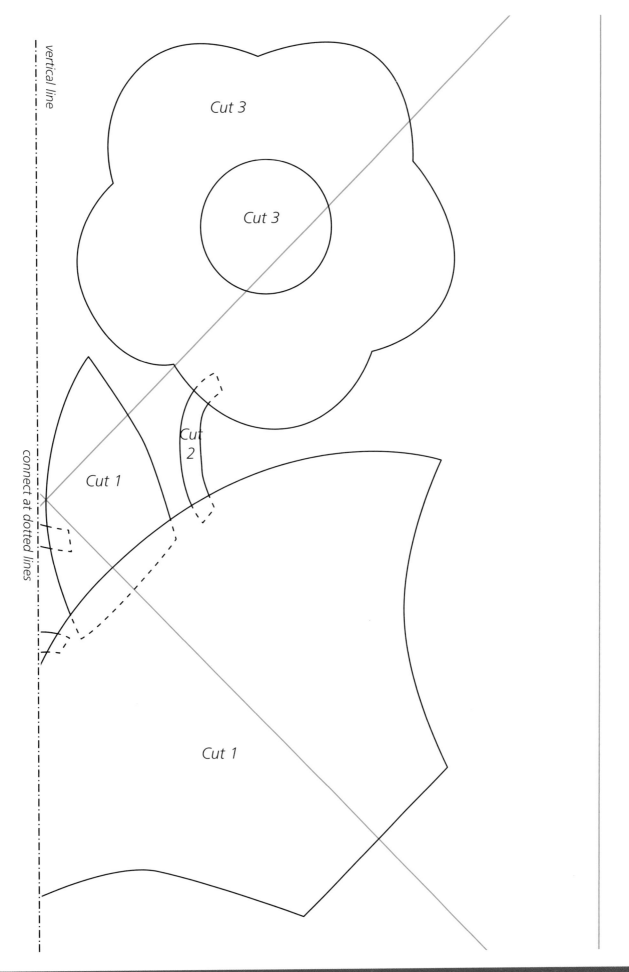

vertical line

connect at dotted lines

Cut 3

Cut 3

Cut 2

Cut 1

Cut 1

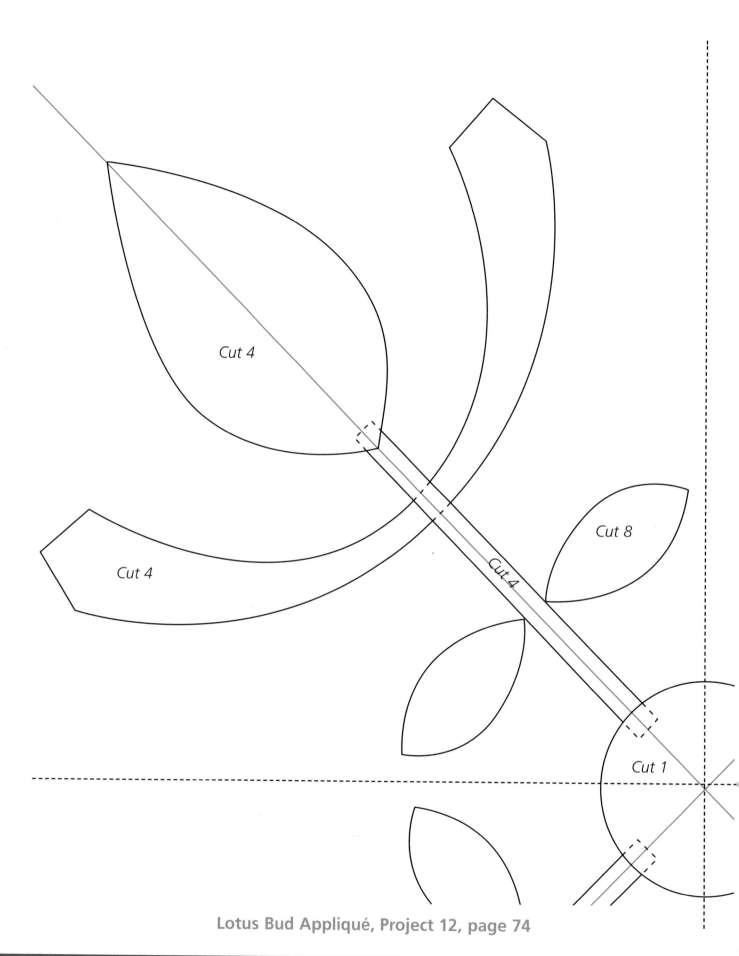

Cut 4

Cut 4

Cut 8

Cut 4

Cut 1

Lotus Bud Appliqué, Project 12, page 74

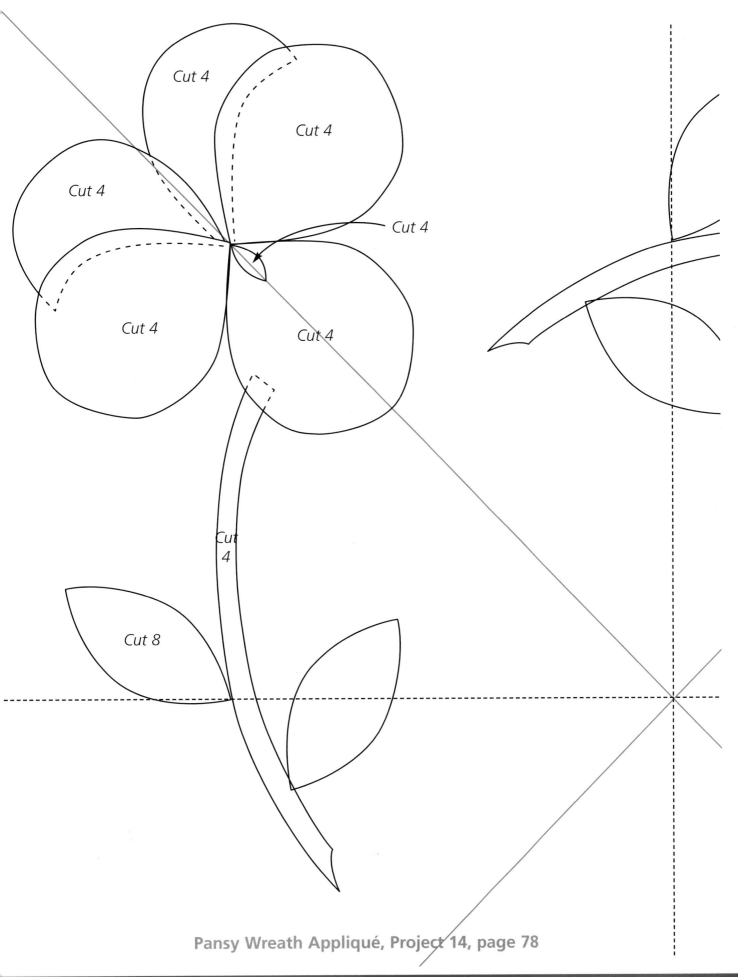

Cut 4

Cut 4

Cut 4

Cut 4

Cut 4

Cut 4

Cut 4

Cut 8

Pansy Wreath Appliqué, Project 14, page 78

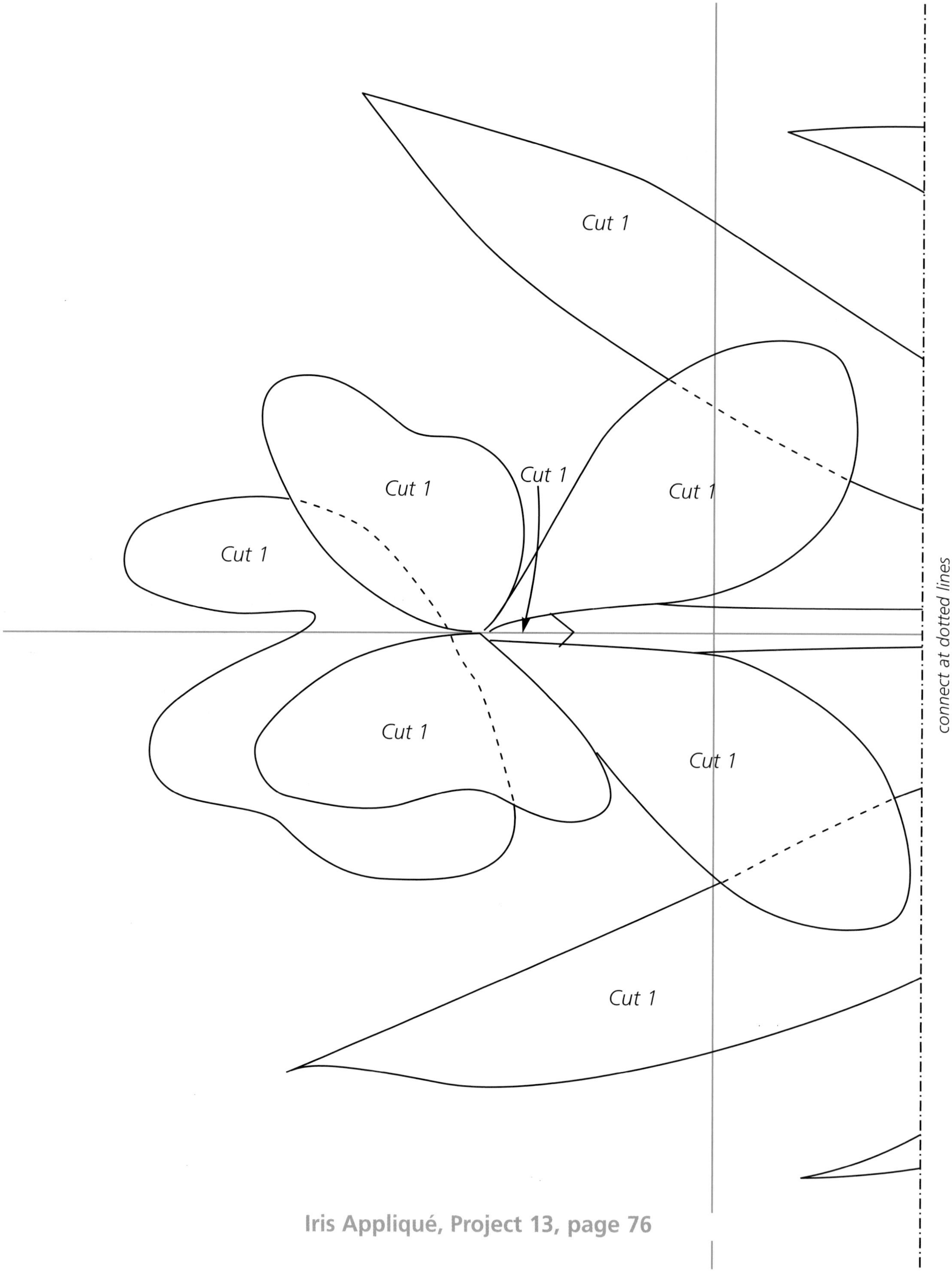

Cut 1

Cut 1

Cut 1

Cut 1

Cut 1

Cut 1

Cut 1

Cut 1

connect at dotted lines

Iris Appliqué, Project 13, page 76

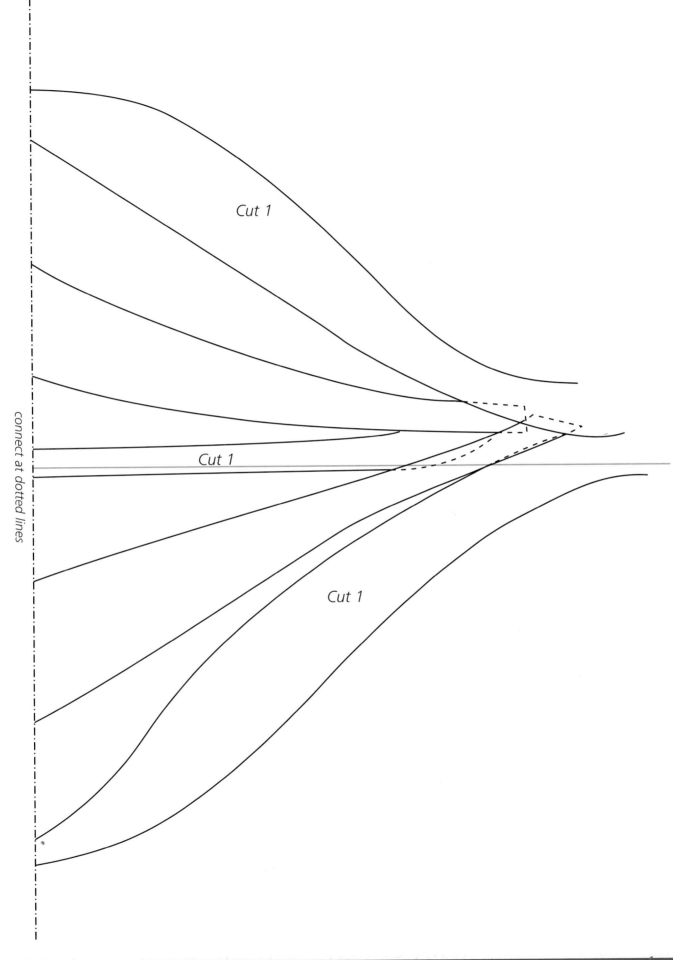

connect at dotted lines

Cut 1

Cut 1

Cut 1

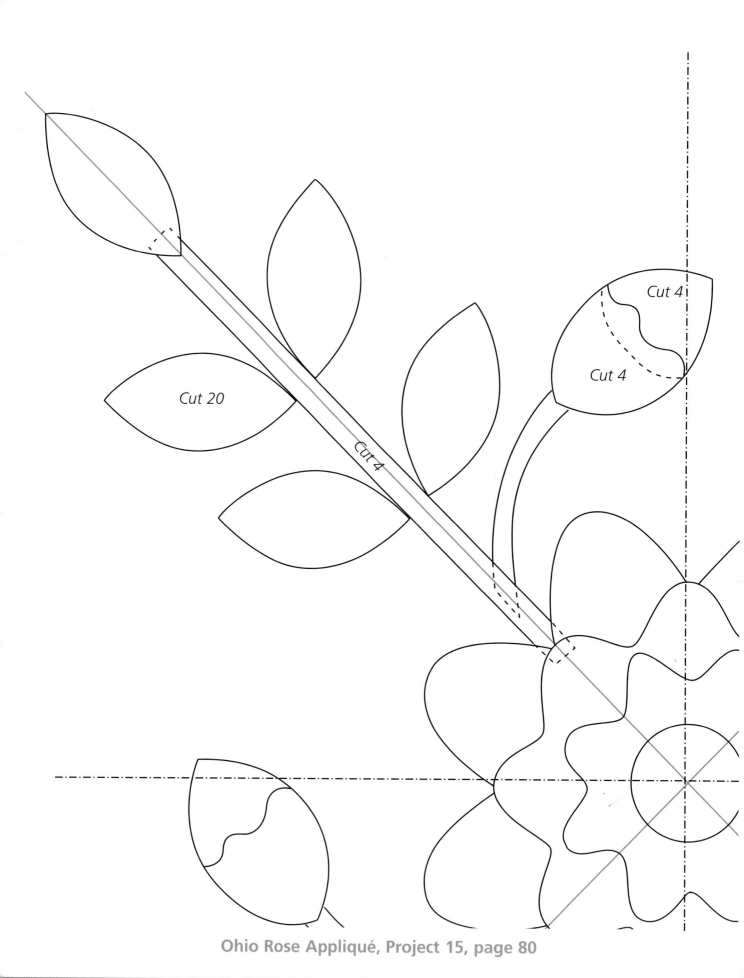

Cut 20

Cut 4

Cut 4

Cut 4

Cut 4

Ohio Rose Appliqué, Project 15, page 80

Cut 1

Cut 1

Cut 1

Cut 1

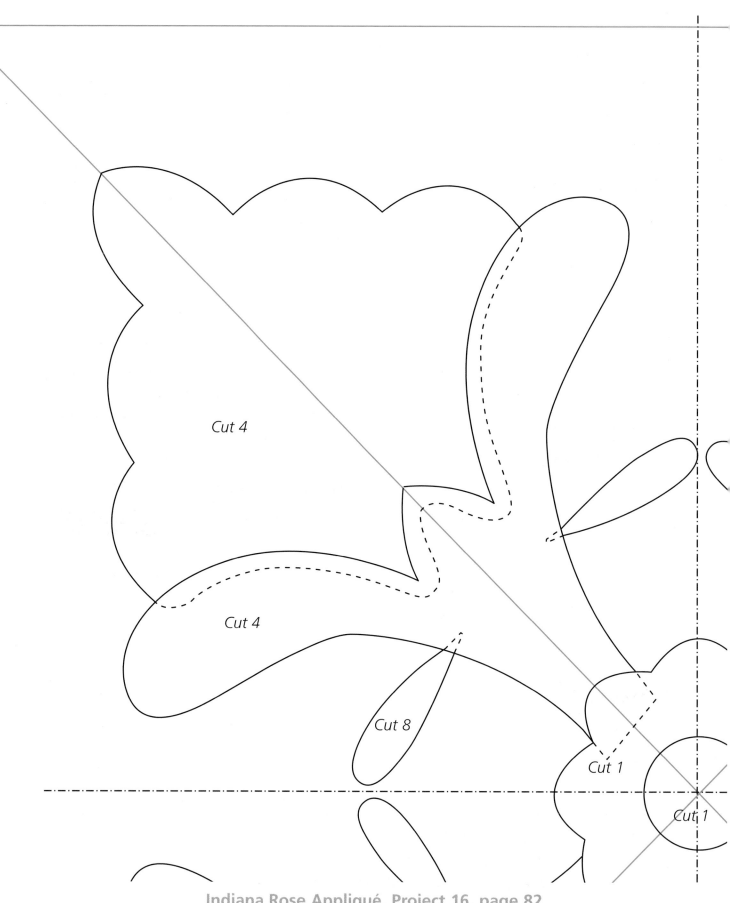

Cut 4

Cut 4

Cut 8

Cut 1

Cut 1

Indiana Rose Appliqué, Project 16, page 82